Eric Rohmer

PHILOSOPHICAL FILMMAKERS

Series editor: Costica Bradatan is an Associate Professor of Humanities at Texas Tech University, USA, and an Honorary Research Associate Professor of Philosophy at the University of Queensland, Australia. He is the author, most recently, of *Dying for Ideas. The Dangerous Lives of the Philosophers* (Bloomsbury, 2015).

Films can ask big questions about human existence; what it means to be alive, to be afraid, to be moral, to be loved. The *Philosophical Filmmakers* series examines the work of influential directors, through the writing of thinkers wanting to grapple with the rocky territory where film and philosophy touch borders.

Each book involves a philosopher engaging with an individual filmmaker's work, revealing how it has inspired the author's own philosophical perspectives and how critical engagement with those films can expand our intellectual horizons.

Other titles forthcoming in the series
Terry Jones, Robert Bernasconi and Jenny Bryant
Alfred Hitchcock, Mark Roche
Jacques Tati, John Ó Maoilearca
Werner Herzog, Richard Eldridge

Eric Rohmer

Filmmaker and Philosopher

Vittorio Hösle

Philosophical Filmmakers

Bloomsbury Academic
An imprint of Bloomsbury Publishing Plc

B L O O M S B U R Y
LONDON · OXFORD · NEW YORK · NEW DELHI · SYDNEY

Bloomsbury Academic
An imprint of Bloomsbury Publishing Plc

50 Bedford Square	1385 Broadway
London	New York
WC1B 3DP	NY 10018
UK	USA

www.bloomsbury.com

BLOOMSBURY and the Diana logo are trademarks of Bloomsbury Publishing Plc

First published 2016

© Vittorio Hösle, 2016

Vittorio Hösle has asserted his right under the Copyright, Designs and Patents Act, 1988, to be identified as Author of this work.

All rights reserved. No part of this publication may be reproduced or transmitted in any form or by any means, electronic or mechanical, including photocopying, recording, or any information storage or retrieval system, without prior permission in writing from the publishers.

No responsibility for loss caused to any individual or organization acting on or refraining from action as a result of the material in this publication can be accepted by Bloomsbury or the author.

British Library Cataloguing-in-Publication Data
A catalogue record for this book is available from the British Library.

ISBN: HB: 9781474221139
PB: 9781474221122
ePDF: 9781474221146
ePub: 9781474221153

Library of Congress Cataloging-in-Publication Data
A catalogue record for this book is available from the Library of Congress.

Series: Philosophical Filmmakers

Typeset by Fakenham Prepress Solutions, Fakenham, Norfolk NR21 8NN
Printed and bound in India

For Barbara and Mark Roche, an ideal couple in love with the arts, with deep friendship

Contents

Preface x

1 The Nature of Contemporary Eroticism: Between Art of Seduction and Nostalgia for the Unconditional 1
   A Very Short History of Eroticism 1

2 *Six contes moraux* 13
   Playing with a Toy and Flirting Aiming at a Third Party: *La Boulangère de Monceau* and *La Carrière de Suzanne* 14
   The Erotic Attractivity of Catholics: *Ma nuit chez Maud* 19
   Narcissism and Promiscuity: *La Collectionneuse* 25
   Rousseauism and Telling on Others: *Le genou de Claire* 30
   Venus and Juno: *L'Amour l'après-midi* 38

3 *Comédies et proverbes* 45
   The Erotic Loser: *La Femme de l'aviateur* 46
   Marriage as Purpose? *Le Beau mariage* 50
   Beach Seductions: *Pauline à la plage* 55
   One Woman, Three Men, and Three Forms of Love: *Les Nuits de la pleine lune* 61
   The Search for the Confirming Sign: *Le Rayon vert* 66

Elective Affinities in an Erotic Quadrilateral: *L'Ami de mon amie* 70

4 *Contes de quatre saisons* 79

Playing the Pander for One's Father? *Conte de printemps* 80
One Man, Three Women, and Three Forms of Love: *Conte d'été* 85
Playing the Pander for One's Friend: *Conte d'automne* 90
Waiting Beyond Rational Hope: *Conte d'hiver* 96

5 The Idea of a Realist Cinema 103

What Does Realism Mean for Rohmer? 113

6 Content and Form in *Pauline à la plage*: Interweaving Words and Images 127

The Imagery of Fall and Redemption 131

7 Rohmer the Non-Moralizing Moralist 145

8 Conclusion 153

Notes 161
Bibliography 179
Index 183

S'il n'y a pas de métaphysique, c'est très artificiel, c'est extérieur, c'est du décor. Cela ne nous touche pas profondément.
If there is no metaphysics, it is very artificial, external, decorative. Such things do not touch us deeply.
Rohmer (2010), 128

Preface: Why Rohmer?

One need not agree with the far-reaching claim that film is itself a form of philosophy[1] in order to recognize that philosophy and film analysis can benefit from each other. On the one hand, film theory often lacks the conceptual precision that rigorous philosophical analysis takes pride in; this holds both for the former's general claims about the nature of film and for concrete interpretations, for example, of moral conflicts, so often depicted in films. On the other hand, the analytical work of pure philosophy is often barren—it teaches a sense for consistency and offers a subtle conceptual apparatus but may well prove unable to connect this apparatus to the concrete moral problems of living people with which great artists are familiar. The reason why many great philosophers have been attracted to artworks in general, and more recently to films in particular, is that they recognize in many artworks cognitive aspirations: the artworks advance claims about the world and about what is right and wrong. Certainly, such claims are much more difficult to grasp than in the case of science and philosophy, for they are hidden in the artwork as a whole, and it would be a naïve error indeed to identify without further ado the artist's claims with some assertions, even philosophical ones, of his characters: for these *belong to* the artwork but do not *express themselves through* the artwork, as the artist does. Still, there is undeniably a cognitive function of art beside the pleasure that it engenders, and it is this function that mainly inspires philosophers. They have to test the artists' claims with their usual methods, but their conceptual tools are often sharpened when confronted with innovative and complex theses, such as those proposed by great artists.

Maurice Henri Joseph Schérer (1920–2010), better known under his pen name Éric Rohmer,[2] is a philosophically fascinating film director for at least five reasons, and thus the right author with whom to start this new series, the central idea of which is to have philosophers, and not film theorists, interpret great film directors. First, after a study of history, literature, philosophy, and theology, Rohmer began his career in film as a film critic, writing, from 1951 to 1963, for the leading French film journal *Cahiers du Cinéma*, which crucially contributed to the formation of the *Nouvelle Vague*, the revolution in French cinema that occurred in the late 1950s and 1960s and anticipated some of the changes that were brought about in the USA by New Hollywood in the late 1960s. Together with Claude Chabrol, in 1957 Rohmer authored a book on (the first forty-four films by) Hitchcock, with whom François Truffaut, another famous *Nouvelle Vague* director, published an important interview book in 1966; in 1972, he added his own chapter to the posthumous edition of the Charlie Chaplin essays of André Bazin[3] and wrote a splendid dissertation on the organization of space in Murnau's *Faust* (published as a book in 1977 and later translated into German but not yet into English). While several other *Nouvelle Vague* directors had a similar beginning (for example, Jacques Rivette, in whose *Out 1: Noli me tangere* Rohmer plays the role of a Balzac scholar), the transition from film critic to film director has not occurred often in the history of cinema. When this transition occurs, however, the films often manifest a greater density of references to the tradition (in the case of Rohmer, not only of film but of literature and painting as well) and a higher degree of reflexivity, an intellectual self-awareness, which is particularly attractive to a philosophical spectator. For while the taste of every artist is based on thought processes, they are often unconscious; and it is rare that someone has such a clear consciousness of his aesthetic principles as Rohmer. Too high a level of reflexivity and too much concern with formal innovations, on the other hand, can alienate a broader audience; the later career of Rohmer's friend, Jean-Luc Godard, whose most famous works are all from the 1960s, is a cautionary tale.[4] Rohmer, whose national and international recognition was much slower than Godard's, nonetheless managed to garner more and more attention for his work, partly because his formal innovations remained constrained by a more traditional understanding of film aesthetics. His originality thus proved to be sustainable over four decades, and he himself to be a modern classic. He certainly succeeded in marking his films with a distinctive style and thus in implementing the central tenet of auteur theory, namely, that the film director must be ultimately in charge of the complex social and industrial process that the making of a film represents.

Another reason for the lasting power of his films is, second, that Rohmer (who in 1946 had published an unsuccessful novel, *Élisabeth*[5]) gives dialogue an extraordinary importance, dialogue (always written by himself) that adroitly mixes everyday topics and the great questions, such as the nature of religion, beauty, friendship, or love. While his screenplays have a high literary quality, and sometimes even are reminiscent of the genre of the philosophical dialogue (which other contemporary filmmaker is able to interweave discussions about grace and freedom or the difference between the transcendent and the transcendental into a completely natural dinner table conversation?), it is the complementary, sometimes contrasting relation between word and image that makes his films great art—a relation reflected by Rohmer himself, who as a film critic did not only write film reviews but contributed to film aesthetics proper as well. In 1955 he published in *Cahiers du Cinéma* five essays on the relation of the film with the other arts under the title *Le celluloid et le marbre* (*Celluloid and Marble*), the republication of which he only allowed a few months before his death. They came out posthumously, enriched by a preface he had written in 1963 for a possible reissue, which did not work out, and by an interview with the almost nonagenary, mentally unimpaired director on this text more than half a century old, the basic ideas of which had been conceived more than six decades earlier. It would be depressing if Rohmer had still agreed with all that the young man had written; but the continuity of his thought is astonishing, and the brilliance of his ideas on the aesthetics of the various arts, formulated in a style of enormous grace and wit, makes this text a classic of film aesthetics. It is a sign of a certain parochialism of much of contemporary Anglo-American as well as German culture that the text has not yet been rendered into these major languages. Important reflections on cinema can also be found in his (unfortunately also yet untranslated) book on the aesthetics of music: *De Mozart en Beethoven, essai sur la notion de profondeur en musique* (*From Mozart to Beethoven: Essay on the Concept of Depth in Music*), in which he demonstrates an extraordinary familiarity with the German philosophical tradition, particularly Kant, Schelling, Hegel, and Schopenhauer. His subtle defense of the special place of film within the contemporary arts is a daunting challenge for all aesthetical theories that neglect film.

In 1963, Rohmer was obliged to resign from the *Cahiers du Cinéma*, mainly because his political, aesthetical, and religious attitude was in marked contrast with those of his colleagues.[6] While most of the *auteurs* of the *Nouvelle Vague* were leftists, if not Marxists, Rohmer was not simply a practicing Catholic; he was even a monarchist. The political controversy that exploded in 2001 over his depiction of the

French Revolution in *L'Anglaise et le Duc* (*The Lady and the Duke*), based on Grace Elliott's memoirs, proved that Rohmer, at least, did not fear to be politically incorrect. But it would be far too simple to condemn Rohmer as a conservative. Even those who evaluate the consequences of the French Revolution as in the whole positive can hardly deny the barbarism of the September massacres and the *terreur*; and Rohmer's conviction that the dignity of a person does not depend on his or her political inclinations but on the commitment to some unconditional moral principle can be appropriated also by people with very different political ideas. Rohmer's conservatism included the desire to preserve nature, and his deep concern for environmental issues was not limited to theoretical pronouncements: he tried to live a sustainable life. His only film about contemporary politics, *L'arbre, le maire et la médiathèque ou les sept hazards* (*The tree, the Mayor, and the Mediatheque*), does not capture the real power mechanisms of modern politics. But its sarcastic indictment of the socialist mayor's careerism can be easily extended to politicians of different political orientations; and its ecological vision remains endearing. It is thus not surprising that, third, even in his most complex films Rohmer's work excels because of his extraordinary rendition of natural beauty. Rohmer's nature is almost never opposed to humans, thus never risks becoming kitschy; on the contrary, it seems to be the natural space for the unfolding of human relationships. But it can inspire people only when they can abstract from themselves and turn, at least momentarily, to a beauty very unlike that of humans.

It is Rohmer's subtle religiosity that, fourth, forms another reason for the complexity of his movies. His religiosity is rarely explicit, as in the films of Robert Bresson, the other great French Catholic film director.[7] Rohmer only rarely depicts religious rites in his films; his characters are mostly utterly secular people. But in their interactions a religious logic seems to be at work that the characters themselves hardly grasp. By that, I do not simply mean that Rohmer is strongly interested in the unintended consequences of erotic behavior; he draws from these consequences moral lessons, which the viewer is invited to consider. Reality in Rohmer is more than a connection of causes and effects; it is suffused with meaning and values. This implies that Rohmer is a moralist; he does not hesitate to render morally wrong behavior visible as such. But the criticism of what he perceives not simply as an error but as a sin is rarely direct; it is mitigated by compassion and supported by an almost sociological view of how the spirit of an age drives the behavior of a person. The commitment to a realistic depiction of everyday life that Rohmer shares with so many of the *Nouvelle Vague* directors as well as with the earlier Italian Neorealists is rooted, in him, in a religious awe for the world and a deep respect for the dignity of each human being. One cannot avoid remembering how Erich Auerbach, in his masterwork *Mimesis*, interprets literary realism as a product of Christian sensibilities.

Fifth, the conservative Catholic, who lived a traditional marriage with a Catholic wife and two children (his son Denis is a well-known leftist French journalist, writing under the pseudonym René Monzat),[8] offers the most comprehensive panorama and in-depth analysis of heterosexual erotic relations in the contemporary Western world that any film director has ever produced. His three great cycles—the six *Contes moraux* (*Moral Tales*), the six *Comédies et proverbes* (*Comedies and Proverbs*), and the four *Contes de quatre saisons* (*Tales of the Four Seasons*)—all deal with erotic problems, as do most of his isolated films, which, however, sometimes reach out to the past—*Perceval le Gallois* to Chrétien de Troyes' Middle Ages, *Die Marquise von O...* (*The Marquise of O*), Rohmer's only film in German, to Heinrich von Kleist's eighteenth century,[9] and his last film, *Les Amours d'Astrée et de Céladon* (*Romance of Astree and Celadon*), to a fictional fifth century seen through the glasses of the seventeenth century author Honoré d'Urfé.[10] Even in the two late works on the transformative historical events of the French Revolution and the global civil war between the two World Wars, *L'Anglaise et le Duc* and *Triple Agent*, the relationship between a woman and a man is as important as the social and mental upheaval. The logic of politics as such is not Rohmer's theme. Probably it is fair to say that Rohmer is interested in the historical background mainly in order to articulate better the mistrust and the moral tensions between the partners and the decisions that they have to make. The three cycles are not simply a twentieth-century *Art of Love* in the medium of film, although seduction techniques are both represented and reflected (after all, talking about seductive strategies may itself be seductive). For, according to Rohmer, eroticism is not simply a technique: it is an event that transforms the personality, is subject to moral principles, and even open to a metaphysical dimension. It is his philosophy of erotic love, his "erotology," that this book tries to distill—not, obviously, by reducing the beauty of his films to simple recipes but by showing how their characters and plots manifest certain truths that Rohmer (as I think, rightly) believes himself to have grasped. The variation of certain themes in the three cycles allows Rohmer to achieve an almost encyclopedic breadth and at the same time reduce the variety of erotic behavior to some basic patterns, for some of his heroes and heroines are "characters" in Theophrastus's sense, that is, ideal types.

The constraints of this series justify why I will focus on the three cycles, rarely quoting from his other films. Since the cycles are so composed that the various films mirror each other, I prefer to go through all of them than to drop one of them in order to have space for some of the isolated films; and in fact, later cycles often refer back to earlier ones, partly because of analogous situations, partly because of the repeated use of the same actors and actresses. True enough, the person played by an actor belongs to a completely different ontological order than the actor himself; but what Rohmer aficionado, when seeing Margot at the beach in *Conte d'été (A Summer's Tale)*, can avoid the happy feeling that he now finally knows what he always wanted to know, namely what type of person the teenager heroine of *Pauline à la plage (Pauline at the Beach)* would become when thirteen years older? For both characters are played by Amanda Langlet. The three cycles can thus be almost called a complex trilogy on contemporary erotic life (it speaks for their unity that they almost completely avoid the repetition of Christian names). Since there is an unfolding from cycle to cycle, and from film to film within each cycle, partly of the development of our sexual mores, partly of conceptual possibilities, I strongly recommend that the person who wants to approach Rohmer's filmic theory of love see the films in the order in which he presents them. My exposition does not necessarily presuppose knowledge of all the films, which I therefore shortly sum up. While a film is much more than its plot, the plot remains its skeleton; and if it is brittle, nothing will be able to flesh it out and transform it into a great artwork.

Rohmer is an intellectual film director with remarkable knowledge of the German philosophical tradition, a master of dialogue, a morally committed admirer of nature's beauty, and a discreet Catholic with a unique glance on the modern world of erotic entanglements. These five reasons validate, perhaps, the interest a German philosopher may take in Rohmer, and my own in particular. The first works I saw by him were the late *Contes de quatre saisons*, but I was immediately struck and began to work my way backward through his cinematographic work. As the author of a book on Woody Allen, I saw in Rohmer a complementary director: in both, the erotic issue is predominant, and both probe the tension between intellectuals and eroticism. But while Allen is a comedian who pokes fun at the absurdities and contradictions of modern erotic imbroglios, Rohmer's austere Catholicism does not allow for a complete desecration of love, as much as he does integrate hilarious scenes in his films. It is not simply that Rohmer avoids the sexual jokes so dear to Allen (jokes that frustrate salacious expectations and therefore are never pornographic); the tone is different. Allen oscillates between comic *joie de vivre* and satiric indictment of human follies; Rohmer's style is elegiac because it points to a lost innocence that never appears on Allen's horizon. The New Yorker Allen does not share the sense for nature that inspires Rohmer, who was born in the small south-central French town of Tulle, and while both authors sneer at many features of the secular world, only in Rohmer is the scorn founded in a religious trust, which Allen may long for but does not possess. As a philosopher who has defended objective idealism as an alternative to both naturalism and constructivism, among many other reasons because it offers a better basis for environmental ethics, who tries to appropriate the spiritual wealth of the Catholic tradition, and who is the author of a large study on the genre of the philosophical dialogue, I cannot help finding myself attracted by Rohmer's work more than by any other contemporary director. But the ultimate reason for my love of his movies is that they capture a rich amount of multi-leveled truths about erotic love, that they point to the possibility of goodness even in erotic love, and that they depict the beauty of nature, of humans, and of the interactions between persons in search of love with elegance and luminosity.

1

The Nature of Contemporary Eroticism: Between Art of Seduction and Nostalgia for the Unconditional

A Very Short History of Eroticism

What is eroticism, and how did it change in the twentieth century? A telegraphic history of its development is necessary, for the contemporary state of erotic relations cannot be understood by way of a subtraction story (to use a term employed by Charles Taylor in *A Secular Age*). It is not simply so that erotic expectations have returned to their "natural" form after the collapse of religious constraints, for there is no human nature independently of its cultural formation, and the history of the human mind remains with us, even when we shake off certain beliefs. A post-Christian culture, for example, differs markedly from a pagan one. What are the main steps in the unfolding of eroticism in the West? In the following sketch, there is a certain focus on French culture, partly because it was particularly creative in erotic matters and partly because it is the tradition from which Rohmer hails.

Sexual behavior was found, as an alternative to asexual reproduction, relatively early in the evolution of life, although it is not completely clear what its selective advantage was, compared with the earlier and less risky form. But perhaps life loves risks, and certainly sexual reproduction considerably accelerated the speed of evolution and facilitated adaptation to changing conditions. Sexual selection was added to natural selection, and in this process life had to develop more beauty if mating was to succeed.[1] In the process of hominization, changes in reproductive behavior must have played an important role. On the one hand, the concealed ovulation in human females detached sexual intercourse from a direct connection to reproduction; on the other hand, the need for bi-parental care increased with the extended childhood of humans. The control of the sexual drive is facilitated by the lack of a specific rutting period; but this also implies a permanent openness to sexual stimulation. The institution of marriage, a commitment to a life in common with the purpose of raising children together, is certainly one of the most widespread social realities among human cultures, even if it has assumed different forms. It always connects not simply two individuals, but two families; therefore, in many cultures, even today, it is not simply a matter that two people alone can decide. Eroticism, on the other hand, is an emotionally very intensive form of preferential relation with another person who gains for oneself more importance than anyone else; it is thus extremely relevant for the formation of a person's identity. The intense wish to be together with the beloved person can, and mostly will, manifest itself in sexual desire and behavior; but this is not conceptually necessary, and there have been intensely erotic but asexual relations. Even less are erotic relations necessarily linked to reproduction and marriage. There is even a tension between eroticism on the one hand and reproduction and marriage on the other. For, first, eroticism consists in the joy of discovery of hidden features, both physical and mental, of an attractive, often mysterious other person, while marriage rests on trust and familiarity; second, erotic love is by its nature a dual relation, while reproduction extends to the younger generation and marrying constitutes bonds with parents and siblings of the partner. It is thus not at all surprising that the first theoretical articulation of erotic love occurs in reference to a relationship that neither leads to reproduction nor connects clans. Greek philosophy of love in Plato's *Lysis*, *Symposium*, and *Phaedrus* is mainly dedicated to male homosexual love, still defended in Pseudo-Lucian's *Erotes* (*Loves*) as superior to heterosexual love; and a large amount of Greek erotic poetry deals with both male and female homosexual love. This type of erotic love could more easily gain autonomy than a love geared toward reproduction. The determination of the borders between friendship and love, the issue of whether one should rather bond with a similar or a different person, the opposition between calculation and passion, the purported advantages of sexual relations without love, and the transformation of erotic desire into spiritual ascent are some of the issues discussed in Plato's dialogues.

One of the relatively few areas where the Roman culture has been truly innovative in relation to the Greeks is the focus of its erotic poetry on heterosexual love, which is presented as the superior form of love in Plutarch's *Erotikos* (*Dialogue on Love*). The high esteem of the Romans for the institution of the family as well as the social and legal status of upper-class women in the late republic explain this change. Catullus, Tibullus, Propertius, and Ovid are the greatest erotic poets of Rome. But while in Catullus and Propertius the erotic passion, harboring contradictory feelings such as love and hatred, is both sincere and destructive, Ovid's *Amores* (*Loves*) are deliberately playful; and his *Ars Amatoria* (*Art of Love*) is a manual of the technique of seducing. As a technique, it can be applied by both sides: the first two books advise men, the third women; and the *Remedia Amoris* (*The Cure for Love*) explains how one can fall out of love again. Eroticism has become a game, but a game that is so exciting because Ovid is also able to depict love that consumes and kills, as, for example, in the *Heroides* (*The Heroines*)—although even in this work wit and irony are not missing, particularly in Helena's letter to Paris, probably the most skillful depiction ever of the initial rejection of a wooing that in the course of its articulation is slowly transformed into whole-hearted acceptance.

Christianity brought forth a sexual revolution by condemning sexual acts outside of marriage, which becomes an indissoluble sacrament, and thus limiting the flourishing of eroticism. Yet the courtly love of the high Middle Ages, which started in southern France partly under the influence of Ovid, led to a new idealization of women unknown to the whole ancient world as well as to the early Middle Ages. The erotic ideal of chivalry is asymmetric: the real power is with men but they have to use it to serve and protect women who inspire noble deeds. The French cleric Andreas Capellanus partly depicts, partly satirizes, in *De amore* (*On love*), this new ideal. In his Essay III 5 *Sur des vers de Virgile* (*Upon some verses of Vergil*), Montaigne, while complaining the injustice that the rules of love have been made by men without consulting women, states that a good marriage should be based on friendship and should avoid erotic love, which has its legitimate place outside of marriage.[2] But clearly, it is only men whose erotic or sexual adventures outside of marriage are condoned—an injustice still defended by as enlightened a thinker as David Hume. The tension between marriages arranged mainly for dynastic or economic interests and the erotic desire characterizes much of the life of the eighteenth-century aristocracy and bourgeoisie, even if Christian ethics enforced hypocrisy with regard to the violations of its norms, at least when women were concerned. The comedy of early modernity, continuing the tradition of Hellenistic and Roman comedy, celebrates the successful attempts of the younger generation to find partners of their own choice against the will of their parents, mostly with the help of astute servants; few works can compete in elegance and wit with the plots of disguising and playing different gender and social roles characteristic of Pierre de Marivaux's comedies. But it is the revolution of authenticity for which Jean-Jacques Rousseau stands that brought the downfall of the bourgeois double moral standard: *Julie, ou la nouvelle Héloïse* (*Julie, or the New Heloise*) of 1761, which probably sold better than any novel before it, is a passionate plea for marriage based on love. The new ideal did not only inspire new forms of love, for it is the nature of deception that it can mimic everything, even sincere passion. Pierre Choderlos de Laclos's 1782 *Les liaisons dangereuses*, an epistolary novel like *Julie*, depicts the most cruel form of seduction that one can imagine. While Ovid teaches the seducer to aim at his own pleasure, the master conspirators Valmont and Merteuil engage in seductive games, which flaunt the newly gained sensibility, only in order to show their utter contempt for moral norms and to destroy naive and even pure persons. In the course of the novel, however, the intimacy between the two anti-heroes breaks down, in part because Valmont proves an increasing attraction for his favorite victim, a married Catholic he succeeds in defiling, and this alienation leads to the ruin of both Valmont and Merteuil. (Laclos is explicitly mentioned in Rohmer's *L'Anglaise et le Duc*, for the author of the novel was later a supporter of Philippe Égalité, one of the two main characters of the film. It is true that the duke speaks disparagingly about the novel but since he hastens to add that he did not manage to finish reading it, and since Rohmer's portrait of the duke is far from flattering, his judgment is hardly shared by the author.)

The cynicism of Laclos's heroes has its roots in a naturalistic vision of reality, which, as in de Sade, can lead to a complete collapse of traditional moral beliefs. Both Rousseau's new sensibility and a metaphysical desolation resulting from the slow evaporation of traditional Christianity contributed to the rise of Romanticism; love is here perceived, on the one hand, as a way to overcome the weltschmerz of religious despair, even if, on the other hand, its normal unfolding increases suffering considerably. Alfred de Musset's 1833 erotic tragicomedy *Les caprices de Marianne* (*The Moods of Marianne*) is one of the masterpieces of French romanticism, and it forms the basis of what is probably the greatest French film ever, Jean Renoir's *La règle du jeu* (*The Rules of the Game*),[3] to which we will have to return. Among the French Romantics, Stendhal has a peculiar position as a narrator, since he anticipates the transition to realism; and the same holds for his greatest theoretical work. *De l'amour* (*On love*) of 1822 remains such a lasting book because it manifests both a post-Rousseauian longing for passion-love, as distinguished from sympathy-love, sensual love, and vanity-love, and a disillusioned penetration of the self-deception that acts in love, the "crystallization" process that transforms even weaknesses into imagined perfections. The mingling of personal concern, categorical differentiation, and sociological overview of the different historical manifestations of erotic love explains both the enduring charm and the insufficiencies of Stendhal's book. The most sober, if not cynical, analysis of nineteenth-century love is offered in Gustave Flaubert's 1857 *Madame Bovary*. What distinguishes it from the two other greatest adultery novels of the second half of the nineteenth century, Leo Tolstoy's *Anna Karenina* and Theodor Fontane's *Effi Briest*, is the complete absence of an admirable couple in the novel, such as the Levins in Tolstoy's and Effi's parents in Fontane's work, and even of an affectionate servant, such as Roswitha. The catastrophe of the Bovarys is inevitable, and it has its ultimate roots in the love novels that young Emma had devoured,[4] building up erotic expectations which poor Charles was not in the least able to match. Whoever remembers that another great hero of modern literature owed his madness to the reading of books,[5] recognizes that romantic love stories are the pendant of chivalric romances, even if nineteenth-century Quixotism lacks the nobility of its seventeenth-century precedent. For Emma, unfortunately, lacks the fundamental goodness that eventually redeems Cervantes' immortal hero. The increasing skepticism regarding the possibility of love does not affect only Catholicism, which, after all, had always taught that the religious life is higher than even marriage. Even a post-Romantic Lutheran philosopher-theologian such as Søren Kierkegaard, who in *Enten-Eller* (*Either-Or*) opposed to the dalliances of non-committal eroticism, which reach their summit in "The diary of a Seducer," the ethical seriousness of marriage, added in *Stadier på Livets Vej* (*Stages on Life's Way*) after the aesthetical and the ethical the celibate religious stage, which is conceived as superior to marriage.

We all live now in a post-Stendhalian predicament—the need for erotic love has increased with the decline of religious beliefs and what set out to substitute for them in the course of the nineteenth century, nationalist creeds. The inextinguishable desire for a community that transcends associations based on self-interest seems satisfiable only in eroticism. At the same time, the spread of a naturalist worldview undermines the possibility of sincerely believing in what one needs.

The tension between exaggerated expectations concerning love, which sometimes even has to replace what trust in God offered traditional cultures (quite a daunting task), and the "scientific" conviction that eros and love are nothing more than cover-ups of sexual drives, is the common background of much of what occurs today in Western eroticism. The most articulate modern defense of a traditional metaphysics and ethics of love—clearly a more comprehensive concept than erotic love, but without a clarification of which erotic love can hardly be grasped as a form of love—in my eyes is due to the Catholic phenomenological philosopher Max Scheler. His book *Zur Phänomenologie und Theorie der Sympathiegefühle und von Liebe und Hass* (*The Nature of Sympathy*) of 1913 sharply distinguishes love from sympathy, interpreting it as perception of values. Values are conceived as something that we do not create but discover; and the carriers of moral values are persons. We will see that Rohmer's basic approach to love is akin to Scheler's even if I do not know whether he ever read him. It is worth mentioning, however, that Rohmer's brother, the philosophy professor René Schérer, wrote a book on the head of the phenomenological school, Edmund Husserl, that Rohmer has a short section on Husserl in his book on music,[6] and that a work by Husserl appears, beside works by Plato, Kant, and Hegel, in *Conte de printemps* (*A Tale of Springtime*). Scheler's influence may furthermore be indirect, since Karol Wojtyła, the future John Paul II, wrote a book on him. Clearly, Rohmer's realism contradicts the subjectivist turn of the later Husserl but is harmonious with the realist phenomenology of the earlier Husserl, to which Scheler remained faithful. In order to understand Rohmer's starting point more in detail, it is imperative to look at some of the changes that took place in the last century and accelerated in the last fifty years.

The most important of these changes is doubtless the emancipation of women. The asymmetry in gender relations that had existed from time immemorial has fortunately been challenged; women have become economically independent, and thus no longer have to rely on men in order to survive. Brutal forms of oppression have been overcome; and even the values of chivalry, being perceived as condescending, have disappeared, although the historical memory of them still haunts sexual scripts. Asymmetry had some advantages, such as rendering superfluous the question of who should make the first step. Indecision increases where both partners are regarded as equal. Still, the demands of justice, which led to greater symmetry, trump all other concerns. The development of effective contraceptives, which were needed to slow down the demographic growth caused by the huge progress of medicine and the decrease of mortality rates, largely detached sexuality from the threat of unwanted pregnancies; this contributed to the fall of the social stigma connected with extramarital, or at least premarital, sexual interactions, the latter often being encouraged by society because they allow people to know each other better before they commit themselves. (This does not exclude that in some limited areas—mainly where symmetry is violated—sexual prohibitions still exist and that their violation triggers compensatory reactions of a vehemence comparable to that of earlier times.) Seduction has thus become a relatively trivial issue; no Western Valmont today can hope to create a great scandal, ruin reputations, and wreak havoc by it. Changes in family law rendered divorce much easier, and the sacramental interpretation of marriage is hardly anymore a lived social reality in the West. Hand in hand with the decline of traditional values, a naturalistic attitude with regard to sexuality spread; the taboos that controlled speaking about it (sometimes even more severe than those checking sexual actions) vanished. Beginning with Arthur Schopenhauer and culminating in Sigmund Freud, philosophers, scientists, and artists began to perceive the pervasiveness of sexual desire in many areas of human culture;

after Darwin's revolution, one could easily understand why behavior directed toward reproduction is so powerful and overrides other concerns, such as moral ones. Sometimes it even manipulates them for its own purposes, such as when the jealous or sexually repressed person indulges in outrage at the sexual behavior of other people in order to satisfy his or her sexual phantasies. With these new insights, the need to discuss and represent sexuality increased. Modesty suffered from it, but no less the mystery that contributed considerably to the aura of the erotic, which now seems only a superstructure of an animal drive. In many aspects, the twentieth century witnessed an inversion of the sexual revolution brought about by early Christianity, and also the rehabilitation of homosexual relations, which become natural when sexuality no longer serves reproduction.

But the human mind knows no complete return to earlier stages. Ovid still believed in divine powers manifesting themselves in erotic desire; the decline of the Christian God did not resuscitate them. Women in the pre-modern world were mostly at the mercy of men; equal freedom is the dominant, if not the only, moral principle of our age. The ethics of authenticity and the increased awareness of one's own special value are not easily satisfied with categorizing erotic needs on the same level as the need for food, which may be taken care of by welfare bureaucracies. The wish to be in control, which stands behind the rise of modern technology, is in strident contradiction with the erotic desire, to which loss of control inherently belongs, superficially during the sexual act, and in a deeper way when one's own autonomy is made vulnerable through dependency on another person's love; and techniques of experiencing the negation of self-control in restricted spaces and time intervals do not solve this issue. The tension between the game of seduction, through which another person is baited and subjected to one's will, and the desire for symmetric love with unconditional trust and thus inevitably also with unconditional obligations, is old. But the fact that seduction has become morally less reproachable, since both genders can engage in it, and that an institution guaranteeing that trust has more or less disappeared (for modern marriage remains precarious due to the ever present risk of divorce), makes it more difficult to achieve the happy ending of the traditional comedy. How does Rohmer react to this situation?

2

Six contes moraux

The first cycle of Rohmer's erotic trilogy differs considerably from the other two. Its first two films—which began to be screened commercially only in 1974—are not feature, but short 16 mm movies; they and the third are in black and white, while all the other films in the trilogy are in color, without which less of nature's beauty can be captured even if the concentration on the acting of persons may benefit from black and white (the third film would have lost its intensity, if in color). What is common to all six of them, and distinguishes them from the later cycles, is the presence of a narrator: Rohmer's texts on which they are based are not dramatic but narrative. Voice-over may sometimes be a cheap device that renders the filming of a scene, and thus the work of the director, superfluous; in Rohmer, this is not its function. On the one hand, it allows an exploration of the sentiments of the main character that cannot manifest themselves in an action or a conversation; on the other hand, Rohmer uses the images that the film adds to the screenplay in order to "deconstruct" the credibility of the narrator. His own narration as a film director, which *constitutes* the story, has to be sharply distinguished from the narration offered by the character, which is *part* of the story, ruthlessly observed by the director.[1] The two can converge if the character has a great intellectual and moral level, but their coincidence is not analytically true.

Several of the narrators of the *Contes* are unreliable, as we will see.[2] The six *Moral Tales* have not only this formal trait in common. They are variations of a situation in which the narrator, a young man who is attracted by, or committed to, a woman, is distracted or tempted by another. (Often the two women form a contrast also through some external trait, such as hair color.) In the first five tales, the attraction or the distraction is encouraged by a friend, usually by a man. Thus, the personal force field of the films is determined by at least four characters: the narrator (N), his friend (F), who can also be an erotic rival,[3] the first woman (W1), and the second woman (W2). Marriage still plays a crucial role—either the hero marries or will marry the first woman that attracted him (Nos. 1, 3, 5), or he is already married and returns to her (No. 6), or it is the distracting woman who marries another, because the narrator is not yet mature enough for marriage (No. 2). It is crucial to study the cycle as a whole; the first narrator's refusal to tell his wife-to-be about his flirtation is exposed in all its shallowness when contrasted with the third narrator's self-effacing honesty. The temptation, in Rohmer's eyes, is not only a danger; since it forces a person to make a choice, there is in it the potential of redemption.

Playing with a Toy and Flirting Aiming at a Third Party: *La Boulangère de Monceau* and *La Carrière de Suzanne*

A low-budget movie such as *La Boulangère de Monceau* (*The Bakery Girl of Monceau*) of 1962 can only have a simple plot, but Rohmer's art consists in endowing it with an enormous psychological depth. The narrator is a university student in Paris; he has eyed among all the passers-by of the metropolis a beautiful and stately young woman,

Sylvie, whose path he occasionally crosses, and they have exchanged glances. The narrator speaks of skirmishes, using a military term for erotic conquest; also his obsession with the geography of Paris manifests an affinity with military thinking.[4] It is, as so often in Rohmer, not the unsuccessful pursuit, which Sylvie too deliberately ignores not to have noticed it, but a fortuitous event that brings N and W1 together and allows the narrator for the first time to speak with her. While she refuses an immediate date, she leaves the possibility open to have it at a later occasion. But then she disappears for weeks. In the bakery, in which the lonely narrator every day eats some pastries, the young salesclerk seems to like him. The connection between gluttony and lust is one of the major topics of the film; but while in Tony Richardson's *Tom Jones* the lunch between Tom and Jenny, which prepares their sexual encounter, is shared by both, at least at the beginning it is only the narrator who eats, a sign of the asymmetric pleasure he is aiming at. Thus he asks for the girl's name (Jacqueline) but does not give his. To take revenge against Jacqueline whose liking for him he takes for granted but whom he ultimately despises for seeming to believe that he could reciprocate it, he invites her out for an evening. But after leaving the bakery, on the way to the café where the girl was told to wait for him, he meets again Sylvie, who had been ill and lives in front of the bakery. He invites her immediately to dinner, selling the bakery girl down the river. Shortly afterwards, the couple marries. The power of the film resides in the contrast between the arrogant self-righteousness of the narrator, who calls ignoring his promise to the bakery girl "moral," while at the same time cowardly fearing a scandal, and the emotional unrest that the camera shows us to occur in the girl. She is for him only a summer substitute for the woman he is waiting for; the scene where he feels her body up manifests that he is both sexually attracted and already bored, when he has partly satisfied his desire, while she for the first time opens up to a man. The film is to a large degree about class—it depicts how from time immemorial males have dealt with girls from lower classes, who are perceived as nothing more than sexual pastries. No less dubious is the relationship between N and W1. For although Sylvie during her first dinner with N claims to have seen all, she has only perceived his gluttony and thought that the narrator was roaming around her house because he had found out her address. Her uncontradicted statement that now she knows all of his vices does not bode well for their marriage (one of the last remarks of the narrator reinforces this impression), even if Sylvie was probably right in not feeling threatened by Jacqueline, inferior in beauty, age, and class. Not that Rohmer ever suggests that the narrator should have married the girl; there was no common basis for that. But Rohmer silently, through the power of his images, denounces how the narrator uses the girl as a toy to be disposed of when something better shows up. The final sentence that he and his wife return to the bakery to buy their bread there but that the clerk

Image 1 Gluttony and lust: The main character (Barbet Schroeder) of *La Boulangère de Monceau*

no longer works there is an indictment not so much of the economy of capitalism as of the mindset that it produces.

The first moral tale still presents a woman in the traditional role of victim. In *La Carrière de Suzanne* (*Suzanne's Career*) of 1963, we have again two young men and two women, but the roles are inverted. Schmidt, the narrator's timid friend in the first tale, is replaced by Guillaume, who is older and far more experienced and enterprising than the narrator Bertrand, whom he instrumentalizes to cover up his affair with Suzanne. Suzanne seems at the beginning merely a victim of the Don Juanism of Guillaume, who humiliates her and even lives at her expense. But in the course of the story, she proves that she can get what she wants: it is she, and she alone, who manages to marry (another character). True, her attempt to have Bertrand fall in love with her fails, and the night she spends in his room does not seem to represent a temptation for Bertrand. But this is not a consequence of him being truly in love with Sophie, the girl he admired before he met Suzanne and whom at the end he loses, too. Bertrand lacks the vital force that the women of various Rohmer films, such as Félicie in *Conte d'hiver*, expect from a man; and his emotional dependency on Guillaume, for which he remains as responsible as Sylvain for his submission to Henri in *Pauline*, blinds him to the point that when money is stolen from him he suspects Suzanne and not his friend, the most likely wrong-doer. It is not clear whether Bertrand's problem is developmental (he is only 18 years old) or characterial; the homosocial bond with Guillaume can be interpreted in different ways. Two topics that reappear in many other of Rohmer's films are already present in the second moral tale. First, the category of "genre" or "type" of person to whom one is erotically attracted is one of Bertrand's erotological discoveries—due to the observation of other people, not to introspection, since he himself has not yet loved. The second issue is that flirting, and even sexual encounters, may well aim at a third party. One may playfully pretend to be in love with a person in order to make another in whom one is really interested jealous; and one may even play the go-between between the person whom one loves but who does not react to one's advances and another. Why so? First, this demonstrates that one really cares for the other; and, second, the failure of the relationship one has helped to initiate may drive the beloved one back to oneself, now with greater maturity in erotic affairs. Suzanne uses both strategies, beside the outright but delicate attempt at seduction in the night that she spends in Bertrand's room; and when she understands that Bertrand is simply not yet mature enough for love, she does not despair but marries her second choice. For she is ripe for the institution, even if this alone does not guarantee that her marriage will last long. Rohmer's second tale is one of his most feminist movies.

Image 2 Shyness and experience: Bertrand (played by Philippe Beuzen) and Suzanne (played by Catherine Sée)

Both women are morally and intellectually superior to the two men. Probably Suzanne herself does not know whether she is naïve or astute: for her ruses are instinctive, and this increases her charm. At least, Bertrand learns to acknowledge the vitality and generosity of Suzanne whom earlier he had pitied in a condescendingly moralistic way, which Rohmer condemns with greater severity than Suzanne's sexual escapades. Bertrand experiences what the hero of the next tale will explicitly claim: that each woman he has been attracted to has opened his eyes for a moral problem that he had ignored and has roused him from moral lethargy.

The Erotic Attractivity of Catholics: *Ma nuit chez Maud*

Ma nuit chez Maud (*My Night at Maud's*) of 1968 is the third moral tale, the first movie that Rohmer was able to make with a real budget and for which he could hire world-class actors.[5] Of all the six, it is the most openly religious and philosophical one; the voice-over is strongly reduced, since the hero tells other people a lot about himself, and the dialogue superb, because it does not simply state the values of the three main ideologies of France at that time, namely Catholicism, Communism, and secular liberalism, but presents them through masterful acting, which fits exactly with their content; the film, finally, is the one that most positively conveys the early Rohmer's vision of love. The four main characters, N, F, W1, and W2, are all round characters—to use E. M. Forster's famous category[6]—while in the first moral tale F (who is absent in the sixth) and in the second, the fourth, and the fifth W1 is flat and two-dimensional. The film is not set in Paris, whose vibrancy the earlier tales captured so well, but in Clermont-Ferrand, during Christmastime, when it was shot.

Rohmer probably wants to suggest that in a small province town the unfolding of lasting relationships has a better chance; but the choice of this specific city, where Rohmer had taught, is also due to the fact that it is the birth town of Blaise Pascal. His books appear twice physically in the film, as Hegel's *Aesthetics* did in *Tous les garçons s'appellent Patrick* (*All Boys Are Called Patrick*), a 1957 short film written by Rohmer and directed by Godard. There, its main function is to poke fun at intellectual pretensions of young female students who are so impatient of erotic experiences that the most obviously lying seducer can easily deceive two of them, who happen to be roommates but discover that they have been tricked with exactly the same phrases only when they see him with a third girl. Pascal, on the other hand, is an important theme of the film. It is his concept of Christianity that the main character, the Catholic engineer Jean-Louis, rejects both in his conversation and in his choice of life; and there is little doubt that Rohmer himself speaks through his hero. For Pascal's Jansenistic rigor, which will recur again in Kierkegaard, cannot render justice to the pleasures and beauties of life; and it is through them, including women, who are more concrete than mathematical problems, that both Jean-Louis and Rohmer believe that one can find God. One may renounce finite goods, but if one does not, it is more religious to acknowledge their positive value—an idea dear also to Max Scheler. Pascal, both metaphysician and mathematician, who in his letter exchange with Pierre Fermat laid the foundations of probability theory, is not only a challenge for the narrator. His old school friend Vidal, whom he accidentally meets, quotes Pascal's famous wager in order to justify his own Communist belief that history must have a meaning: it is rational to bid for something very unlikely but having a probability larger than zero, when the stakes are infinite. It seems to me that the main result of Vidal's appropriation of the wager is to discredit it in Rohmer's eyes; for if Pascal's wager can be used to justify all sorts of beliefs that exclude each other, it cannot work. (One might object that the secular appropriation should not be allowed to assume an infinite stake; but the problem remains, since there are different religions, who threaten the adherents of other religions with eternal damnation.) Jean-Louis furthermore declares that what he dislikes in the wager is the idea of exchange, of buying a ticket like in a lottery. One cannot approach God in this way.[7]

Jean-Louis, who has lived from his childhood with the certainty of having God within himself,[8] has returned after several years in the Americas and relationships with four different women, which, as he probably correctly claims, never lacked love, to France. While attending mass in the Romanesque basilica of Notre-Dame du Port, he observes a young couple whose faith and affection to each other touches him; and then he eyes a beautiful single woman (Françoise), whose devotion is striking and whom he suddenly decides to marry. The desiring glances with which he observes her do not pass unnoticed, even less when he pursues her with his car; and her irate turn toward him in the church as well as her smile on the street betray the ambivalence of her feelings. Moving from eye contact to talk, however, proves difficult, and so Jean-Louis accepts Vidal's invitation to a Christmas dinner at a local free-thinker's house. Maud is a beautiful and intellectually brilliant divorcée, Vidal in love with her, but a short amorous relationship has proven that their characters are not compatible. No doubt, one of Vidal's motives in bringing Jean-Louis to Maud's house, where he leaves him alone with Maud after the dinner, is to see how she will react to him; thus, if she begins an affair with him, as Maud later explains, enabling him to have a pretext to hate and despise her, who does not reciprocate his love. But Vidal's revenge proves to be subtler than his intentions probably were: Maud is soon infatuated with Jean-Louis, whom, however, she proves unable to seduce either by the unveiling of her soul or of her body. Jean-Louis is erotically strongly attracted to her, and due to the lack of another bed they spend a night in the same bed, Maud even being naked. Only in the morning does Jean-Louis become willing to oblige, but then Maud pushes him back, insulted that he waited so long. Why does Maud fall in love with the narrator, and why does he not react? Maud is emotionally fascinated by what is utterly different from her and what at the same time she wants to conquer, because she regards it as inferior to her way of reasoning; Jean-Louis, on the other hand, is determined, first, that from now on he will have a relationship with a woman only when he wants to marry her and stay faithful to her, ideally for love, but if not for self-respect,[9] and, second, that he can only marry a Catholic woman, because love is easier where there is community of ideas. Love and religion reinforce each other. Maud cannot even consider conversion, even if Jean-Louis suggests it; her family practiced irreligion as a religion, and even if she claims to be indifferent toward religion, she hates the hypocrisy connected with much of it, and which she believes she senses in Jean-Louis himself. A further reason for her antipathy is that her marriage broke apart, because both she and her husband had lovers, his being a young Catholic woman, whom she hated with all her heart, even if the sincerity of her love was undeniable. With unerring female instinct, she furthermore feels that Jean-Louis is in love with a woman who is Catholic herself. Vidal, on the other hand, although an atheist, who states that he enjoyed his best sexual experiences in short non-committal encounters during conferences, remains attracted by Christianity; he grants the sublimity of the couple observed in the church as well as the charm that religion confers on women: in search for women, one should indeed go to mass (where, Maud grants, one finds less ugliness than in the cells of the Communist Party). Up to this point, the plot of the story might confirm only certain tenets of the sociologies of religion and family: a common religious background tends to grant more stability to relationships, and the suffering of children from divorce can be considerable, even if Maud denies it. But in dealing with her daughter, to whom she cannot mediate the meaning of Christmas, even if she drowned her with presents and adorned her house with an utterly artificial Christmas tree, Maud lacks maternal warmth; children like hers or Henri's daughter Marie in *Pauline* seem to be mainly perceived as threats to their parents' autonomy. France has had a long tradition of atheist or agnostic Catholicism, from Auguste Comte to the Action Française of Charles Maurras, whose metaphysical skepticism did not prevent him from recognizing the relevance of religion for the maintenance of the social order.

But what makes *Ma nuit chez Maud* such a subtle film is that the bond that finally is forged between Jean-Louis and Françoise is based not on the recognition of the utility of religion but on a common spiritual experience. The message of the Christmas sermon—that the incarnation has to be internally appropriated by each Christian—inspires both figures. He addresses her, without formalities and following an urge, for the first time after the night at Maud's when he happens to see her in the street; and he meets her again, by chance, after a second encounter with Maud (which he uses to take leave from her; unlike the narrator of the first tale, he keeps the appointment made the day before). Circumstances oblige him to spend a night in Françoise's dorm, but not in her room; and when he enters her room again because he is looking for matches, the unwelcoming attitude of Françoise, whose head rests beside a cross, is the perfect contrast to Maud's seduction attempt. They have already dated several times when, on the snowy hills over Clermont, Françoise confesses to him that she had an affair with a married man. Jean-Louis, who had declared to Maud that what counted for him was not the single act but the life as a whole and the purity of the heart with which one lived it, and had earlier tried to convince Françoise, who was tormented by remorse, that not to hope in Grace was a sin, is in fact relieved; for now they are in a situation of equality, even if Françoise insists that her guilt is greater, since her lover was married. To reassure her, Jean-Louis confesses to her that he himself had slept with another woman the night before he met her (something true according to one of the two meanings of "sleep"), and he has to promise her never to speak about the issue again. For unlike Maud, Françoise shies away from delving into one's past. Years later, the narrator is vacationing with Françoise and their son on the beach, a place that will become more and more relevant in Rohmer's films. Suddenly, they meet Maud again, and only now, based on the encounter of the two women, Jean-Louis understands that it was her husband whom Françoise had loved. (Even this is not explicitly said but left for the

Image 3 Françoise (played by Marie-Christine Barrault) confesses to Jean-Louis (played by Jean-Louis Trintignant) her earlier relation

viewer to infer.) He has the tact and the love to pretend not to grasp this, and the final shot captures the young family running together into the sea, while the beautiful, seductive, haughty, and ultimately lonely Maud, whose second marriage is falling apart, has to recognize that two of the men she loved were lost to the same woman, whose faith in a religion, which does not deny the reality of sin among Christians but knows ways of forgiving, remains unintelligible to her. It remained alien to many critics, too, who, deceived by the fact that the four main characters all have something to hide and express their inner conflicts by exquisite facial expressions and movements, were unable to see the difference that Rohmer is drawing between the successful couple and the two other persons.[10]

Narcissism and Promiscuity: *La Collectionneuse*

La Collectionneuse (*The Collector*) of 1966 is Rohmer's first film with Néstor Almendros as cinematographer; even if still made with a minimal amount of money, it was awarded the Silver Bear Extraordinary Jury Prize at the Berlin Film Festival. The success of the movie was partly due to its unbiased depiction of open promiscuity among the young generation—while Bertrand had to keep Suzanne's ultimately innocuous presence in his room over the night secret, the new heroine, Haydée, is not at all discomfited by the fact that the narrator, Adrien, meets her for the first time in a friend's villa while having sex with another man. When later, spending the summer vacations together with him in another villa in Saint-Tropez, she disturbs his sleep by loud sex with changing partners, not only is she not embarrassed, but she seems amused. There are good reasons why traditionally people have not desired witnesses to their sexual encounters; if they are expressions of dual intimacy, there is no reason to address a third party. When someone wants to be distracted or at least cherishes the thought that he or she is distracting someone else, there is no longer true intimacy, and sex is not an expression of love. There could hardly be a sharper contrast between Haydée, who in the first images is presented as a Venus rising from the sea, with a perfectly beautiful body, and the guilt-ridden and loving Françoise of the third tale cowering on the beach after the encounter with Maud, letting sand run through her hand, both an expression of her remorse and a symbol that time might heal. But even the structurally corresponding seductress figure of Maud, intellectual, selective, and not easily approachable, is as distant as possible from this pagan goddess, who at the beginning seems to stand for nature and an insatiable sexual urge. She collects males, as others do objects. While Haydée exceeds all earlier women by her animal-like sensuality (she rarely speaks), the new narrator outdoes all earlier male characters by his narcissism and intellectual pretensions; and doubtless Rohmer dislikes him even more than Haydée, for Rohmer loves nature, even if a return to it is precluded to any human being. Even Haydée cannot simply drift like the waves of the sea but is entangled in a struggle for recognition; unfamiliar with the emotions of love, she oscillates between sexual drives and abstract will. Adrien's aim for the vacation is to do literally nothing, to reach absolute nothingness—slogans known from the French existentialism of Jean-Paul Sartre and Albert Camus. His friend Daniel has similar ambitions, even if in a more energetic and brutal way. He is a painter, who has reached fame by creating, for example, a yellow pot adorned with razor blades; the critic who touches it gets cut by it but is enthusiastic because he now can boast of frequenting dangerous people. W1 appears only shortly in the last of the three preparatory scenes, when Adrien, his girlfriend Mijanou, and Annik discuss love and beauty. Mijanou declares something beautiful because we love it. The aestheticist Annik defends the inverse relation: she can entertain even superficial relationships only with beautiful people, because she perceives all ugliness as an insult, and her drama is that she only rarely meets beautiful persons. The film is an early satire of empty intellectualism, formalism in the arts, aestheticism without love, and promiscuity, phenomena that all began to dominate Western Europe in these years; and the three disconnected prologues, which introduce the main characters, so contrasting even in their colors, formally correspond to the feeling of broken unity that the film is about. The organic unity of the third tale is lost; but since the object of the fourth is the loss of order, there is a harmony between content and form, which somehow repristinates the aesthetic unity.

The value of the movie does not lie simply in the cinematography that captures the beauty of the Provence landscape, of the sea and the light in a way that contrasts with the tortuosity of the three main characters; it is rather the unfolding of the psychological triangle between Haydée, Daniel, and the narrator, who are alone in their friend's huge villa. Both men, who can barely hide their desire for her body, still treat Haydée with an intellectual condescendence that wraps itself up with phrases from Rousseau; and this resistance elicits Haydée's obstinate wish to seduce the narrator. He is not wrong in perceiving it, even if Haydée vehemently denies it, but he is insincere in not conceding that he shares her wish on an emotional level even if, as a matter of will, he has decided not to yield to it because he does not want to be added to her collection. Still, the erotic attraction between him and Haydée is unmistakable; in this matter, the body language is a more reliable witness than a censored stream of consciousness. While it was Vidal who pushed Jean-Louis toward Maud, whom he himself desired, it is now Adrien who asks Daniel to have sex with Haydée, and while Daniel first refuses this type of service, he and Haydée then engage in visible intimacies. The problem of such all-too-open encounters is that they are mainly sending a message to a third party, *for whom* they are taking place; in general, many of the interactions between two members of this film's group are stage-actings directed at the third. This cannot but leave Daniel unsatisfied, whose abrupt departure is owed to the fact that once he has been added to Haydée's collection and has whetted Adrien's appetite, in the eyes of the young collector he has become uninteresting.[11] The acting becomes even more explicit when Sam appears, a collector who wants to buy from Adrien a Song vase; he is attracted to Haydée, and Adrien leaves her overnight at his house, departing under a pretext. The situation is somehow reminiscent of Godard's *Le mépris* (*Contempt*) of 1963; but while there Camille breaks with her husband, because she feels that he wants to use her beauty to ingratiate himself with the producer, Haydée, who, after all, is not married to Adrien and seems to oblige without resistance. When Adrien returns, Sam and Haydée play the couple, but it is too obvious that they play it. When Sam humiliates Adrien, Haydée breaks the enormously valuable Song vase—unlike Prince Myshkin in Dostoyevsky's *Idiot* it seems on purpose; with this act she declares that she does not care for collections (or rather that she wants to add to her collection the man who despised her for being a collector). Adrien is touched and willing to become for a limited time her lover but on the way back to their villa, when she is contacted by old friends, he suddenly decides to leave her and returns to Mijanou, whom at the beginning he had refused to join in her travel to London.

In both the third and the fourth tales, the gender roles are traditional—the man is more reflective, the woman more naïve and natural. But while Jean-Louis and Françoise share a common faith, which can become the cornerstone of a common life, the opposition of the genders in *La Collectionneuse* is extreme. Haydée's actions are

Image 4 Adrien (played by Patrick Bauchau) shows for the first time his appreciation of Haydée (played by Haydée Politoff) after she broke the Song vase

certainly more instinctive than deliberate, as well befits this symbol of nature, while Adrien's uninterrupted self-reflection does not allow him to behave naturally. The fact that ultimately he does succumb as little as Jean-Louis to the seduction has nothing to do with the reasons that constrain Jean-Louis; his motives are the wish to impress Daniel and win in the power struggle with Haydée; vanity and pride, not moral principles or love, impel him. Whether the sudden inspiration at the end connects him with grace or is another twist of his narcissism remains an open question. In Rohmer's eyes, the collapse of a common value order must give way to a naturalistic form of living human sexuality, on the one hand, and narcissism on the other; reciprocal humiliations and power struggles will replace love. If the greatness of a mind is measured by both its width and its capacity to maintain consistency, then one must recognize that having created two films that are so different in form and content from each other as are the third and the fourth tales but still offer the positive and negative articulation of the same conviction was an early proof of Rohmer's genius.

Rousseauism and Telling on Others: *Le genou de Claire*

In *Le genou de Claire* (*Claire's Knee*) of 1970, we never see W1 in the reality of the film (only a picture of her is shown); instead, W2 is doubled into two teenage stepsisters. Since they both keep the hero, Jérôme, busy, F can be a woman, the writer Aurora, whom he no longer seems to desire erotically, even if he often touches her; but in a culture that cherishes gallantry and likes to distribute kisses, it is not easy to demarcate conventional friendship between man and woman from erotic desire. The difficulty is increased by the fact that not every woman is appreciative if she is perceived only as a human being, and thus some compliments may even originate in, or receive a rationalization as, a charitable impulse. The fuzziness of the limit emerges most clearly at the end, when the hero can finally touch and rub Claire's knee, satisfying his strong erotic desire and thus liberating himself from it, while making Claire believe, or at least making himself believe that Claire believes, that he is paternally consoling her. (Like several of Rohmer's male heroes, he suffers from partialism, the favored organ being the knee. It is appropriate to read partialism as a consequence of the incapacity of perceiving a person as a whole; if one only looks at the body, it shrinks itself to a part.) Even in the internal perspective it is not always clear when a desire is sexual in nature and when not; and Jérôme, narcissistic, vain, and loquacious (brilliantly played by Jean-Claude Brialy), is never honest with himself and never takes responsibility. He exemplifies to the highest degree what Sartre calls "bad faith."[12] Aurora is partly a confidante, to whom this would-be Don Juan, who in truth resembles more closely Don Quixote, narrates his embellished adventures, and partly a manipulative figure, who uses him as a guinea-pig for her own narrative purposes. (Famous is the scene where through a sudden withdrawal movement she has Jérôme almost touch Claire's knee.) Her smooth combination of affability and merciless observation of weaknesses is the mark of the artist—needless to say, also of Rohmer himself. Jérôme's reports and Aurora's comments render the voice-over superfluous; but the film is still an artwork in which narration is as important as action, even if now the deconstruction of the narrator's perspective is not left to the audience but is partly rendered explicit in the film itself. Narration becomes part of the dramatic interaction between characters, as in the so-called mixed dialogues, already present in Plato, such as the *Euthydemus*, which form a third type beside the direct and the indirect dialogues.[13]

Jérôme, a French diplomat and cultural attaché, has returned to the Lake of Annecy to sell the villa where he spent his childhood, since he is about to marry and now lives in Sweden. While driving with his motor-boat under the Pont des Amours, he is eyed by chance by his old friend Aurora, who has rented a room in the villa of a lady first widowed, then divorced (she herself tends to confuse the two types of loss, against her daughter's protests). She has both a daughter, Laura, and a stepdaughter from her second marriage, Claire, who comes to visit later in the film. She likes to sigh that her error was to have loved too much, while the modern generation will be happier by not believing in love anymore. The city Annecy is known to every Rousseau reader from the second book of *Les Confessions* as the place where he met Françoise-Louise de Warens, who played such an important role in his sentimental education; and clearly the name of the lady, "Madame W..." in the text (178), alludes to her, as does the cherry tree scene of the film to the analogous one in Rousseau's main autobiographical text.[14] The closeness of Lake Geneva reminds us also of *Julie*, since the film ironically reflects the novel's love-relation between a teacher and his pupil. The other theorist of love whom Rohmer, well familiar with German culture, has in mind is Friedrich Schlegel: for the name of Jérôme's bride is Lucinde, and that is the title of his famous, at that time scandalous, 1799 novel that pleaded, like Rousseau's *Julie*, for love marriages and even taught that the emotional bond rendered the juridical form of marriage superfluous. Clearly, the film is an attack against the Romantic inflation of love; and Rohmer shows masterfully what the main problem of the new doctrine is: it teaches people, and particularly men, to look not at their partner but at their own sentiments; the ultimate consequence is infatuation with one's love, not with its object. While Adrien suffered from an excess of will, Jérôme is afraid of willing and wants to keep the volitive element in love as small as possible, and thus elude any duty and obligation; instead, Rousseau's pupil enjoys "delightful sensations" connected with "rural pleasures." Marriage is for him no special commitment; he will marry Lucinde, with whom he often split up, because he is by now accustomed to her. Since few figures in early Christianity have so much fought for asceticism as Saint Jerome, the name of the narrator can only be in ironic contrast to him, if the identity of the names is not completely coincidental. The name Aurora, while an homage to the Romanian actress Aurora Cornu, who plays her, perhaps shall also remind us of Nietzsche's famous work, which wants to challenge the prejudices of morality—for the name in Latin means "dawn."

In his first encounter with Laura's mother, Jérôme confuses her with another person; and he does not even understand that Aurora is about to marry herself. When she leaves for several days, he does not really care why, and when she introduces him to another man, he does not realize that he is her fiancé. For Jérôme has difficulties grasping that a woman may be in love with some other man. His dalliance with Laura is for him only a condescending flirtation with a bobby-soxer, whom he pretends to teach his wise outlook on love, while amply using the occasion to feel her "amicably" up; he even tries to kiss her passionately but is pushed back by Laura, who would like to be sincerely loved by a mature man but feels that he is only faking passion. (He will later ascribe responsibility for this kiss to Aurora.) First, Jérôme declares Laura to be completely naïve, although Aurora warns him that today young girls are no longer ingenues (in fact, Laura tells her mother that there was not more love earlier, only more hypocrisy); later, not concerned with consistency, he reassures her mother that Laura is only playing. As in *Pauline*, Rohmer sides with the younger generation, whose idealism is not yet destroyed by the cynicism of the parent generation but who at the same time try seriously to understand what is going on among the grown-ups. Despite her nervous giggling, Laura, whose name evokes Petrarch, is psychologically enormously perspicacious; and we think even of the mythical Leda when swans approach her while sitting at the lakeside. Laura truly loves and trusts her mother, she knows that her own longing for an elder man is due to the loss of her father, and she is aware of the fact that falling in love may be nothing but a flight from boredom. No doubt, she enjoys the flirtation, from which she gains more than Jérôme, since she is less experienced and wants to learn. But her interest in the topic of love, and to a lesser degree in Jérôme, is existential; and the curiosity and volubility of the flirtatious bridegroom will probably do her more harm than good. Their conversation soon addresses some great questions, such as the relation of friendship and love, crucial also in later films. Laura opposes friendship to love, for the latter renders her mean. This is a sign of her lack of maturity, for her meanness results from her incapacity to deal with emotions that overwhelm her, because they endanger her autonomy; she is afraid of beautiful boys, as she feels oppressed by the beautiful landscape, and detests their triumphalism when they can vaunt a conquest. Jérôme, on the other hand, declares that he does not believe in love without friendship. This remains true despite the shallowness of the character; it is one of the basic insights of Rohmer, repeated again and again. But friendship is a *necessary* not a *sufficient* condition for love; additionally, erotic attraction is needed, which is inevitably selective. Jérôme's explanation that beyond a certain level all women interest him equally and that only the moral or mental factors decide is a grotesque self-deception, as we will see when Claire appears and he immediately begins to neglect Laura. The statement about the moral factors, however, is involuntarily, and thus comically, correct, for Claire is not only far more beautiful than Laura; her character is stronger, and the strength of her character is manifested in the grace of her motions. For as Laura rightly says, echoing a remark by Jean-Louis, the moral can only become visible through the physical. While Jérôme deceives himself concerning the specific factor of erotic attraction, he is honest but wrong regarding the third element of successful love: commitment. He teaches his apprentice that lovers must respect each other's freedom, which is not false; but he does not consider that the limitation of future freedom through commitment to each other may be the highest form of freedom. He even explains to Laura that he flirts with her only in order to prove to himself that he still likes Lucinde. While it does not go without saying that Lucinde would like to hear this, it is obvious that his remark hurts Laura. But Jérôme does not care about, and probably does not even perceive, this. For the man is too narcissistic to be cruel. Cruelty, after all, presupposes empathy.

Image 5 Jérôme (played by Jean-Claude Brialy) gets attracted by the knee of Claire (played by Laurence de Monaghan)

Claire, clear as the waters of the lake, is intellectually inferior to Laura but emotionally ahead of her through her experience of love. The contrast between the two girls is marked by the different colors of their clothes: red for Laura, blue for Claire. Her commitment to her boyfriend Gilles is without reservation and was probably never based on the deliberate weighing of alternatives; and this torments Jérôme for three reasons. First of all, he is physically attracted to her in a way in which he never was to Laura, something which the latter immediately perceives in the cherry tree scene by observing Jérôme's lecherous leer at Claire's well-built leg. Observations of second order, i.e., of the observations of other people, occur often in Rohmer's films; they usually proceed from women, who probably perceive more quickly than men when they become, or cease being because the male attention has turned elsewhere, the subject of erotic desire. Jérôme feels pure desire: that is, he is excited by his own excitement without any concrete interest in Claire's person. The desire for desire replaces the love for the person. (Adrien, analogously, exercised pure will—he wanted to prove his strength of will without willing any concrete object.) Second, Claire is as uninterested in Jérôme as a person can ever be; she does not even care to show it. This hurts his vanity, for he does not want to do the first step in a courtship—another issue that reappears in various later films. The narcissistic personality is not willing to run risks. At the same time, Jérôme says that he would despise Claire if she ran after him—a situation somehow reminiscent of the statement by Groucho Marx, who did not care to belong to any club that would have him as a member. And indeed, Claire would lose much of her dignity if she lowered herself to the level of Jérôme. Jérôme is not simply jealous of Gilles, he is envious of him, the difference being that he would not like Gilles to be loved by a person such as Claire, even if he himself had nothing to lose. And in particular he is, third, envious of Claire. For he himself is unable to love as Claire does, and when he tries to destroy her love, he is driven by resentment, a phenomenon so well analyzed by Nietzsche and Scheler as the wish to denigrate values that are not accessible to oneself. When he pompously declares to Laura and Aurora that Gilles is far beneath Claire, he projects unto Gilles what he feels about himself. But he reaches the pinnacle of his meanness when he says the same thing to Claire, in the famous scene when they seek cover before the rain under a shed. That two persons of different sex seeking shelter from the weather in a covered place may develop erotic feelings for each other is a well-known topic, treated already in the fourth book of Virgil's *Aeneid*; the dangerous situation makes people cling to each other, and the rain is a tempting metaphor for ejaculation. But the only means of approaching Claire that Jérôme finds is railing against Gilles; and when she shows him her contempt, he tells her what he just witnessed—that Gilles whom she supposed traveling was in town embracing another girl. Jérôme does not make up the scene, which he perceived through his binoculars—just as the audience of the film descries only a small image within his binoculars. The binoculars are a powerful symbol of his voyeurism, which contrasts with commitment (a topic so well explored in the sixth episode of Krzysztof Kieśloswki's *Dekalog* (*The Decalogue*)). Claire sobs desperately, and this gives him, who at the beginning had declared that the weeping of women disarms him, finally the occasion to touch her knee. He leaves the next morning, with the sincere conviction, similar to that of the narrator of the first tale, to have done a good deed by having alienated Claire from Gilles. But after he has left, Gilles arrives, and Claire trustingly asks him what he did yesterday. Gilles has a good explanation; he could not travel, and then he met an acquaintance whom he consoled since she was in a crisis. The couple are quickly and happily reunited. Whether Gilles is lying we do not know; but it is Claire who has to find out, and we wish the two good luck. Jérôme, the only hero of the *Contes* who is not present until the end of the story, does not perceive his defeat; but who cares? The sincere love of two youngsters is incomparably superior to the self-complacency of an intellectual only in love with himself and intent on subverting passion when he discovers it. Quite near the beginning, Aurora answers Jérôme's question in the negative whether she ever considers using his character in one of her stories; and when he inquires whether this has to do with him being so dull, she confirms but adds that one may write good stories about insignificant people. One has to concede both the general point and the concrete application: Rohmer's film is perfect, even if only due to the inclusion of Aurora, Laura, and Claire. *Ma nuit chez Maud* is more profound, but the grace of *Le genou* can hardly be surpassed.

Venus and Juno: *L'Amour l'après-midi*

Frédéric, the hero of the last story, *L'Amour l'après-midi* (*Love in the Afternoon/Chloe in the Afternoon*)[15] of 1972, is the only one already married at the beginning; the threat is thus that of an adultery. The greater gravity of the act, and the more complex strategies of seduction that thus become necessary, explain why this tale completes the series: a closure also achieved by the appearance in the dream sequence of the six leading female characters of the last three tales. (It is a revenge of the malleable Laura that the only woman who is able to resist Frédéric is played by Béatrice Romand, who played her role in the earlier film and will return in four other Rohmer movies, while the couple played by the actors of Claire and Gilles are quickly split by Frédéric, who proves thus more powerful than Jérôme.) While W1 here is almost as round a character as in the third tale, F is missing—or perhaps one could say that F is replaced by the colleague Gérard, who declares to be "practically faithful" to his wife (why not simply faithful?), and the initially amused and increasingly worried witnesses of the seduction attempt, the two secretaries of the two lawyers. Frédéric's wife is called Hélène, the temptress Chloé: both Greek names, and while the first refers back to the Spartan queen abducted by Paris, the second, which means "young foliage," may allude to the bucolic novel by Longus from the second century, *Daphnis and Chloe*. The two women represent institutionalized and erotic love respectively (Juno and Venus), the contrast between which already Montaigne described. Rohmer demonstrates masterfully in the "Prologue" how the real temptation becomes possible only because Frédéric is bored by his diligent wife, who never comes to his office and whom he takes too seriously to speak openly with her about his innermost concerns. Thus, he spends much of his time with erotic phantasies, phantasies that are facilitated by his subway readings of Bougainville[16] and the many non-committal encounters with people whom one will never see age[17] offered by a metropolis such as Paris, the dynamism of which replaces the sea and lake landscapes of the two precedent tales.[18] With a word from Robert Musil, we could call Frédéric, as other heroes from later films, an erotic "Möglichkeitsmensch" (person of possibility). On the one hand, he resents that his marriage has inevitably meant a narrowing down of the real horizons of his bachelor time. On the other hand, the marriage extended his mental horizons—for before his marriage only some women qualified as possible partners, due to the category of genre or type already discussed; now, however, he no longer classifies women into elect and reprobates but each one seems beautiful and fascinating. The idea that marriage weakens the sense of erotic exclusion, which the interest in a type entails, returns in *Conte d'automne*. It is probably psychologically correct, for when one has gained and come to know what one wanted to have, one may face possible alternatives that once were only second choices; and the inevitable disappointing of some expectations naturally triggers second thoughts. At the same time, Frédéric is not an active womanizer: his oscillation between family life and career does not leave him the time and energy necessary for that. His daydream of owning a device that would allow him to impose his will on women replaces the active quest; and his infantile desire of what is logically impossible—to live both first loves and lasting loves—shows that he probably would limit himself to permanent mental adulteries and some flirtations, as those with his secretaries, which he enjoys because both sides know where to draw the line that demarcates the private and the professional. When the young au pair who helps with his small children bolts naked out of the shower as soon as she hears the baby cry, he is slightly disconcerted; but despite her youth, he is not really tempted. After all, an affair is demanding, and why undergo such stress if the phantasies extorted by the abundance of Parisian women are sufficiently satisfying? (One might maliciously add: even if probably not as satisfying as writing and filming stories about erotic temptations. The similarities between Rohmer and his hero are obvious.)

In a great artwork, even small details contribute to the organic unity of the whole; and of course Frédéric's shopping tours, in which he tries all possible clothes but chooses none, symbolize his attitude toward women. When, however, a beautiful salesclerk shows complete indifference regarding his choice, he is seduced into buying a shirt he did not really need. This is the same strategy Chloé will follow. Her success in tempting Frédéric is the more surprising, as she had been the girlfriend of one of his friends, and he had worked hard to liberate him from her devastating influence. It is likely that she enjoys a certain revenge in bringing Frédéric to the same degree of dependence; but there is little doubt that at the same time she is sincerely attracted to him. And this for the same reason why he is attracted to her: they represent two opposite sides. Frédéric stands for order, bourgeois marriage, and hard work; she is unable to live a lasting relationship, and changes jobs as often as men. A Dionysian force emanates from her, which Frédéric cannot resist when she appears in the afternoon, the most difficult time of his biorhythm. One could compare Chloé almost with Boudu in Jean Renoir's *Boudu sauvé des eaux* (*Boudu Saved From Drowning*). Rohmer's art is most evident in indicating the gradual steps by which Chloé gains power over her victim, appearing in ever new clothes before him and sometimes visible to us in the office's mirror, a symbol of Frédéric's relentless imagination and his narcissism. Her first appearance annoys him like that of a ghost; he does not want to remember that once they had even played lovers and refuses to offer her a job. Her subtle revenge—bringing him presents for his children—humbles him; and he finds this woman increasingly interesting, who both mocks his bourgeois life and would like to join it. She creates a certain complicity by having Frédéric help her with practical problems: once he is considered her boyfriend by the landlady; once he even violates a law by helping her to break into her former partner's apartment, where she insists that he take down photographs taken of her in attractive positions. Representing herself as desperate and close to suicide, only held alive by the hope of a child, who would belong to her alone and not to the father (for children are the only hope in this world), she increases Frédéric's care for her; and the contempt with which she speaks about her various boyfriends (whose beds she shares because she needs one) gets across the message that she is looking for something better, while it invites Frédéric to speak about his wife too and so to loosen the special bond that connects spouses. While initially complimenting Frédéric on his wife, Chloé pokes fun at him for fearing her and for demonstratively repeating how much he loves her only because he feels obliged to do so. By once asking him whether he refers to his wife or his secretary, she undermines Hélène's special status. Later, she will even tell him that she spotted Hélène with another man.

The ruse reaches its summit when she declares that she needs his presence at an evening dinner to ward off an admirer; and when he says that he could not explain such an absence to his wife, she entices him to lie to her, using the sophism that since he has not told her about their afternoon encounters either, this is nothing new. He complies, but then she cancels their appointment on the day it is due, obliging him to lie a second time to his wife (who now understands that she has been fooled). Frédéric begins to feel jealous of Chloé, and she confirms to him after her return that she had left with that admirer, whom she then, in order to take her revenge against what men had done to her, suddenly left for a teenager, who, however, did not elicit lasting maternal feelings. She then announces to him that her old decision to have a child completely for herself has matured further: for she now knows that Frédéric will be the child's begetter. The fact that he does not immediately reject the idea and does not break off contact evidences that he is hooked. After a meeting in the clothes shop where Chloé works and where she tries all possible outfits in front of him, he visits her twice in her apartment, and the second time she welcomes him, coming naked out of the shower and asking him to rub her with a towel. Since his jacket scrapes her, she demands that he take it off, and he is now determined to take the rest off too, when, while pulling his sweater over his face, he suddenly remembers that he has done the same thing with his children at home to amuse them. It is this memory of his family life, and perhaps also the conviction that the child about to be begotten would most probably live a very different life, with no father and a mother with no sense of responsibility, that suddenly, like a flash of the light of grace, brings him back to his senses. He runs out of the apartment and returns to his wife. The last scene shows, on the one hand, that

Image 6 Frédéric (played by Bernard Verley) is reminded of his family while taking off his sweater

Hélène had understood very well in what danger their marriage was; earlier, her glances at Frédéric the one time that he told her about Chloé displayed a complete knowledge of her husband's emotional trial and confusion. They reconnect, even if Frédéric does not make a full confession, which his wife would not like to hear, for their marriage is based on maintaining a certain distance and respect for the partner's intimacy. Even if Frédéric complained to Chloé that he and his wife played roles to each other, Rohmer suggests that human fragility needs masking; it is the brutal openness of Chloé that destroys every lasting love. Even marital love needs politeness. And Rohmer embodies the same delicacy by limiting himself to discreetly alluding to the couple's withdrawal to their bedroom where they will express their regained love and trust.

3

Comédies et proverbes

The *Comédies et proverbes*, all from the 1980s, differ from the first cycle through the disappearance of the voice-over; when the narration of one's erotic adventures occurs (for as always in Rohmer, dialogue and reflection are more important than mere action), it is always directed to another person in the film. The male predominance of the first cycle is replaced by greater symmetry between the genders and even by a stronger focus on the women, who are now often the ones who choose. The new films have less thematic unity than the first six tales; the proverbs or verses at the beginning of the films have no common theme, and are sometimes only ironically connected with the story they precede. Rohmer names as a further difference the fact that the new heroes debate less ultimate ends and more the means to get there; and this makes these figures more touching and frail.[1] Indeed, there is no equivalent to Jean-Louis and Françoise in this cycle, no explicit discussion of religious issues; the only scene in a church that we witness is when the most calculating person of the whole cycle, Sabine, prays for the fulfillment of a selfish wish, which will not be granted. Religion has waned, the secular ideology of Marxism has disappeared; even Rousseau is no longer read. The main erotic categories now are "mec" and "nana," boyfriend and girlfriend; the taboo on premarital and even adulterous sex has become obsolete;

and marriage has ceased to be the normal goal of a relationship. Even if some of the heroes succeed in forging relationships which we hope will be stable, none of them is married or about to marry (even if they may have an affair with a married person or be divorced themselves); and the only one who directly aims at marriage fails miserably and deservedly. Children from divorced marriages have become frequent. The social pressure to be sexually active is enormous: the deviant is now the one who refuses to subject herself to it. Laura no longer possessed the enigmatic and thus touching mixture of naiveté and erotic desire and curiosity that characterized the pre-modern teenage virgin, but her successor, Pauline, is far savvier in erotic affairs, while at the same time lacking the trust in first love that embellished Claire. All these changes have indeed occurred in the 1970s, and Rohmer captures them with his usual precision. Since the nature and architecture that surround this new generation remain splendid, since Rohmer feels empathy for all his characters, and since some of them are truly good persons, all of these films are enlightening. But not all are masterpieces. For even if the aesthetic value of an artwork is mainly a function of how it represents reality, the intrinsic poetic value of the reality depicted cannot be ignored either, and one has to recognize that the latter value has decreased in the second cycle.

The Erotic Loser: *La Femme de l'aviateur*

La Femme de l'aviateur (*The Aviator's Wife*) of 1981, shot in 16 mm, but later blown up to 35 mm, presents a woman, Anne, who is entangled in four different types of relationships with men, and the torments of her five-years-younger lover, François, a student. He witnesses in the morning that she has been visited by her ex lover, the aviator Christian, who in fact has informed her that he wants to break off their relationship and return to his wife (who gives the title to the film but never appears in it). But François is jealous and when he later by chance sees Christian sitting in a café with another woman, he follows him. His not exactly professional behavior as a sleuth elicits the curiosity of a fifteen-year-old girl, Lucie, who for some time joins him in his pursuit. When he returns to Anne in the evening, she tells him the truth but goes out with another man. François sends Lucie a postcard, even if he has just found out that she is the girlfriend of one of his colleagues. Two connected topics dominate the film: first, the fleeting nature of erotic relations in contemporary Paris, and second, the voyeuristic interest in the erotic life of other people. Clearly, the two strands belong together. For the person truly committed does not have time to play the voyeur and, trusting the partner, does not spy on him or her. Who is not committed, on the other hand, rarely has a partner who is committed her- or himself; and she or he is motivated to observe erotic behavior partly by jealousy, partly because she or he is on the lookout for something better. Anne's problem is that she cannot chose; not only is she torn between Christian and François, but she is also courted by a certain Mercillat, who is happy to have heard the rumor that she is about to marry an aviator, because her supposed husband's frequent absences would allow him to visit her more often, and by Carrère, who still addresses her in the V form "vous" and with whom she goes out in the evening. François explains to her that the latter simply wants to be seen with a beautiful woman; it is thus a case of vanity-love in Stendhal's terminology, while Christian's love qualifies as passion-love and Mercillat's as sensual love. Her love for François is a case of condescending sympathy-love; she does not mind hanging around, and occasionally sleeping, with him, but uses every occasion to make clear to him that he is her last choice. (She told him about Christian as her Prince Charming, but never mentioned that he was married, for this could have reassured him.) One has the impression that François is most useful to her when she can triumphantly tell Christian (who declares to be so sorry to have to dump her, mitigating it by the empty declaration that he will always love her) that in fact she might have dumped him first, since she had just spent her vacation with François. Anne's basic value is absolute freedom for her affections. When François generously states to her that she has the right to love Christian (who, as she had earlier said herself, is free to love whomever he prefers), she is furious because nobody has to grant her rights, since "everything is my right." This does not prevent her from becoming jealous when François tells her about Lucie, while at the same time warning him that the trick to render her jealous won't work. In her discussion with her friend Sylvie, she insists that for her loving someone and wanting to live together with him are two completely different things, that she prefers to be unhappy alone rather than lose her autonomy, and that she is not so old as to have to think of marriage. Sylvie, on the other hand, tells her that marriage is natural when one has a lasting feeling for a person, that marriage is a beginning not an end, and that her own various boyfriends were only steps toward the final choice. Anne, however, lacks the predilection for a certain type and tries all possible men. Lucie can hardly believe that Anne loves two men as different as Christian and François, who concedes that her random choices are particularly shocking for him. Anne never senses the sincere affection that François has for her, who at the end will not tell her what he has observed, even if she discovers that he is hiding something and that he cannot be thinking of nothing (this is the content of the initial proverb, which varies Adrien's futile attempt at doing nothing). In marked contrast with Jérôme and later Pierre in *Pauline*, François does not tell Anne what he saw his rival Christian doing, the meaning of which remains ambivalent to the end; he only mentions Lucie, not so much to render Anne jealous but to save her the pain that the full story might comport. Still, she reproaches him for seeing only his little problems and never thinking about her.

Lucie is physically and intellectually as different from Anne as are the two settings in which we mainly encounter them—the large Buttes-Chaumont Park for Lucie, a narrow apartment for Anne. But Lucie, too, plays with François. The daughter of "amiably divorced" parents is an excellent observer, again of the second order like Laura, but unlike Laura stating it explicitly, and she follows François while he is stalking Christian and the unknown woman. His lies to her are so ridiculous that she soon finds out what is going on. The situation amuses her, for she likes life when it seems like a novel. Although she reproaches François to make cinema out of his love story, she contributes to it by trying to motivate an Asiatic couple of tourists in the park to take a picture of Christian and his female companion. The hilarious attempt to involve an unknowing third party in the sleuth activities fails, but Lucie gains more and more information about François without reciprocating in the least. For, as she is right in telling him, the fact that someone unveils his erotic secrets does not entitle him to hear those of the other person. Her mockery becomes increasingly more biting, particularly when, seeing a picture of Anne, she affirms that the two do not fit together—even if she later adds that she never found a couple fitting. The main lesson that she wants to give François is that it is always the woman who chooses the partner— something Anne cannot agree with in her partly melancholy, partly hysterical last scene. The film is one of Rohmer's most somber ones. Anne, who complains that she has returned from the coiffeur with "the same head," is unable to change her self-destructive behavior; even her self-perception is minimal. Lucie is far more intelligent, but the uncanny sagacity that she exhibits with regard to love activities is frightening for a girl her age. Poor François is caught between the two women, who are emotionally stronger and/or intellectually subtler

Image 7 Lucie (played by Anne-Laure Meury) asks the Asian tourist (Neil Chan) to take a picture of her, hoping in vain that the picture will also frame Christian (played by Mathieu Carrière) and his blond companion (played by Haydée Caillot)

than he is and exploit and manipulate him respectively. It is difficult to be optimistic regarding his future: he is a born loser, for he truly loves. Traditionally, this position was rather assigned to women, but Rohmer suggests that the scales may have turned. In the fourth film of the series, however, we will see the male revenge.

Marriage as Purpose? *Le Beau mariage*

If an erotic situation in which both partners reserve the right to look around for alternatives and the greatest fear consists in not having been the first to dump the other is, at the least in the long run, emotionally slightly less satisfying than it promised to be, one might want to return to the good old institution of marriage. That is what Sabine thinks, the heroine of *Le Beau mariage* (*A Good Marriage*) of 1982. In many aspects, she is the reverse of Anne; while the latter was dominated by her fleeting desires and feared marriage, Sabine forms the abstract decision to marry—yet without knowing whom. (That distinguishes her from Jean-Louis, of whose strength of will she is a grotesque caricature.) She reminds us of that Heidegger pupil who after reading the chapter on resoluteness in *Being and Time* stated that he was absolutely resolved to act but did not yet know what to do. Despite their different outlook, the two heroines have something in common. For as Anne had in Sylvie, so Sabine has in Clarisse a wise friend, who lives in a stable relationship and knows that one first has to find one's personality before one can develop it; she is married and thus can be a model for Sabine. In order to help her and also because she likes to play the role of the matchmaker (a role that Jean-Louis claimed to detest but which becomes increasingly important in Rohmer's films, partly to facilitate the "famous first steps"), Clarisse brings Sabine in contact with her cousin Edmond, a prosperous lawyer. After their first meeting, Clarisse proclaims to have witnessed a "coup de foudre," the electrical discharge of love at first sight.[2] However, the castle-building does not succeed. But why, if marriage is the right institution for erotic love, as the Catholic Rohmer never failed to believe? Two factors have a bearing on the outcome. First, Edmond does not want to oblige when he feels the pressure that is put on him by Sabine's family; he just came out from a stormy relationship, and wants now to concentrate on his career. Furthermore, as he bluntly tells Sabine, he is not in love with her, even if she corresponds to his type (of which, as Clarisse told Sabine, he had already gathered quite a collection of women). Marriage, after all, cannot be decided by one side alone, and Sabine is less world-wise than her mother and Clarisse, who understand that men are no longer easily convinced to marry. For they can have girlfriends at considerably less costs, and economically Edmond and Sabine do not belong to the same class. Success in seducing a man for a night does not guarantee success in seducing him into a yes for life, even if Sabine is so convinced that she will be able to find Edmond's weak point that she quits her job and announces the marriage as a done deal. Nevertheless, she will reject as an insult Edmond's insinuation that she desired marriage when her hopes are scattered.

Second, the problem is not simply Edmond. For Sabine has even more in common with Anne than the relationship with a more mature girlfriend. True enough, her decision to no longer let herself be loved because of her buttocks is a sign of self-respect, and the insight she shares with her mother that modern women have forgotten that male desire quickly abates without female resistance is, while not exactly original, correct. But when she adds that she wants her lover to suffer —something Marion will repeat in the next comedy—the question arises that Pauline will pose to Marion: why does one want someone to suffer whom one pretends to love? This is precisely the problem. Sabine is as selfish and loveless as Edmond, and while some common traits may well be a necessary condition for a happy couple, they are clearly not a sufficient one. Two people who love solitude, but also two people who love only themselves, are hardly a good match. The relationship between Sabine and Edmond is symmetrical, unlike the one between Anne and François; but this alone does not make it a happy one. It is furthermore not immediately obvious why a person should enjoy the privileges of marriage whom at the beginning we see making love in an atelier with a married painter, with whom, however, she breaks it off because she is hurt that he takes the phone to greet his child, who has just returned from a vacation and to whom he explains that he cannot see him this evening since painters work through the night. Not that Sabine's decision to discontinue this relationship is wrong; what is wrong is that the reproaches against her partner are not accompanied by any self-criticism. She is an arriviste, as her first boyfriend (the only one, as she confesses Clarisse, she could have lived with) tells her. By chance, they meet in the splendid Romanesque-Gothic Le Mans Cathedral. Claude is surprised to encounter her in this place, but she tells him that she has changed—another instance of her lack of self-awareness, for nothing in her heart has been altered, only her immediate aim has been shifted. Rohmer makes clear that true religiosity does not side with Sabine, who lights a candle and demands something for herself, but rather with Claude, who calmly contemplates the glass windows and declares that he prays without asking and believing. We will see how, in the last film of the next cycle, Rohmer's critical attitude to petitionary prayer is modified.

Rohmer would not be a complex artist if his Sabine lacked any insight. When she insists that a woman perceives the beauty of her lover when he works, not when he parades before her, since this usually renders him ridiculous, she indeed recognizes that a lasting relationship cannot circle around itself; each partner must have an encounter with the outside world and respect the partner's relation to it. Her remark that love presupposes some effort of the will is not wrong either, but it is as unilateral as Jérôme's complete denial of the volitive element. Clarisse exaggerates when she declares that her marriage was only a concession to social life; but she is right that the will can only reinforce love, it cannot create it. The artificiality of Sabine pretending to be in love with Edmond is grotesque; and the open hatred into which this pretended love changes in the final encounter between the two in Edmond's legal office is scary, even if Rohmer manages to channel Sabine's aggressivity into an action against a female client of Edmond's who suddenly comes in: one of

Rohmer's funniest scenes, also due to Edmond's sorrowful exculpation that his *profession* obliges him to receive all sort of people. The saddest thing about Sabine is her unwillingness to learn from her failure. Her incapacity to mend her ways is expressed by the similarity between the first and the last scenes of the film, which show her in the train between Le Mans and Paris—the two cities between which the action oscillates. At the beginning, she and an attractive young male passenger look quickly at each other, but not at the same time; after the collapse of her marriage hopes, she deliberately sits down in front of him, and the film ends with both exchanging glances and smiles. We recognize that she is determined to slide into the next relationship (probably now without hope for marriage) with no pause for reflection. It might be helpful to contrast her behavior with Corinna's in Theodor Fontane's 1892 novel *Frau Jenny Treibel*.

Image 8 Sabine (played by Béatrice Romand) asserting herself in the church

Although sentimentally connected to her cousin, Corinna manages to engage secretly with a wealthy young man, whom she does not love but whose lifestyle she covets; however, her hope to marry him fails due to his mother's resistance. In this situation, in which she risks to lose both men, she is grating rolls in the kitchen with such a wrath that the old housekeeper of her widowed father, Schmolke, comments that she seems to want to destroy the whole world. And when Corinna confirms, Schmolke adds: "Yourself included?" It is her answer "Myself first and foremost" that signals to Schmolke that Corinna has understood where the fault lies.[3] This leads to the novel's happy ending, with Corinna finally marrying her cousin. True enough, today's marriage decisions take more time; wise and affectionate old servants no longer grace many households; but the lack of a happy ending in Rohmer's film has mainly to do with Sabine's personality.

Beach Seductions: *Pauline à la plage*

Neither Anne nor Sabine are lovely persons, because neither knows the commitment of love; and both films about them suffer from a certain didacticism, which becomes flesh in the female friends and Sabine's mother. The third film, *Pauline à la plage* (*Pauline at the Beach*) of 1983, is the jewel of the cycle (to which we will return later in more detail) for the main heroine, the beautiful Marion, neither juggles with four relationships at a time nor is determined to marry a rich man; she is a divorcee who hopes to have finally found her true and only love. Her self-deception is almost beyond belief; but her heart is nobler than that of Anne and Sabine, and so the film is comic rather than satiric because it elicits more compassion than contempt. But the main reason for the film's excellence is the replacement of the mature friend Sylvie/Clarisse by a much younger confidante, Marion's teenage cousin Pauline, whose grace enlivens this story as much as Laura and Claire invigorated the plot of *Le genou de Claire*. The film has six characters—three men and three women. Henri and Pierre belong to the same age group as Marion: Sylvain is a teenager like Pauline; furthermore, there is the candy seller Louisette, who belongs to a socially lower class but sex with whom is defended with the argument that one has overcome social prejudices. (Indeed, the times of the bakery of Monceau are gone.) Everything could peacefully work out for the erotic needs of a summer vacation in Normandy, and for Marion beyond them, if only Marion were willing to settle for her old friend Pierre, who has always loved her, Henri satisfied himself with Louisette (neither of them is too choosy concerning sexual playmates), and Pauline and Sylvain could continue their making out. But deeper feeling on the one hand, boredom and intrigue on the other, come in the way. As much as Marion has always liked Pierre amicably, she is not erotically attracted to him, while she falls for Henri, who manages to get into her bed the night of the same day they meet on the beach. But Henri is quickly bored, clearly in part because the lack of autonomy and self-control that Marion displays hardly induces respect. Not only does he also have sex with Louisette, he disappears after a few days with another woman, after having tried in vain to rape Pauline shortly before. First, however, he manages to sour the budding relationship of Pauline with Sylvain by pushing him, who happened to be in his house, with Louisette, with whom Henri was just having sex, into his bathroom, where they are discovered by Marion, who comes by for a surprise visit and is horrified by the level of persons with whom her young cousin is hanging out. Only later is he obliged to confess the truth, but not to Marion. This is the simple plot, and it is amazing what Rohmer was able to make of it through dialogue and acting as well as through the use of the camera. The reason why the skeleton of the plot blossoms into such a splendid film is that humans do not simply mate like animals. Even such a simple endocrinological-hydraulic phenomenon as a nocturnal emission is usually accompanied by a dream, that is, a mental event; and the heroine, Marion, can have sex only if she convinces herself that she has found true love. A long and deep discussion on love at Henri's villa is needed before Henri can seduce Marion. Henri is an anthropologist living in Oceania; he stands for lack of roots and bonds.[4] A self-declared nomad (though with quite an impressive sea-front villa), a man who does not want to give an account of what he does to anyone, he claims to dislike even furniture and does not allow any woman to treat him as such, not even the mother of his daughter, who is with him for a few days before he can send her back to her mother, with the justification that children need roots. Marion is fascinated: for she, too, hates being attached to a man—however, not to any man but to a man for whom she does not burn. Alas, while people have burned, perhaps even committed suicide for her, she herself has not yet experienced the flame of true love, which as such inevitably desires to last for ever; she only believed that she had succeeded. But people have a right to err, and she now waits for the *coup de foudre* that will set her ablaze. Pierre warns her that such fires do not last long, but Marion counters that she wants to walk from surprise to surprise and not think ahead. Pierre, not unlike Kierkegaard, points to the temporality of love, and Henri takes his chance to agree but reduces temporality to the present. Pierre, he complains, forgets living while thinking of an unlikely future, for like Marion he is waiting for something. Pierre declares that he does not wait for a flame, but for a durable love on which one can rely. The three different concepts of love—Marion's romantic, Pierre's sober, and Henri's hedonistic one—are not simply theoretical constructs; they emanate from the personalities of their defenders, and while they are speaking it becomes clear that they are at the same time tools of erotic conquest. Marion is desperately searching for a new partner and projecting her expectations into Henri; Henri seduces her by demeaning Pierre, who visibly has Marion in mind when he speaks about his desire not again to live with a woman whom he does not really love, such as the one from whom he just split. Artfully, Henri invites Pauline, who has seriously listened, to join in the discussion. She is hesitant but then declares that love presupposes knowing a person,[5] that friendship and love are related, that love is not a dream or a subjective imagination but a slow approach to the depth of a person: by far the most mature analysis, produced without pretensions and hidden agenda. This does not prevent the three adults from treating her and later Sylvain with extreme condescendence—Marion will confide to Pierre that these teenagers are all dull and brutal.

The contrast between sexual needs on a summer beach, heightened by the huge amount of bare flesh that displays itself, and the emotional and intellectual pretensions with which people cover them is an important topic of the film. Needless to say, Rohmer does not want to bolster a naturalistic attitude toward love, such as that represented by Henri, who is probably honest when claiming that he is not a Machiavellian but acts without reflection. Still, I believe, Rohmer thinks that a person who is so outright about his sexual desires as Henri, while more dangerous, is less ridiculous than Marion. The day after their first night, when Marion raves about her passionate love for Henri—something that never had happened to her before—and the abashment that she now feels in front of Pauline (who already found out what she hoped to hide from her), Henri answers her question whether he reciprocates her sentiments in the affirmative, but with so little enthusiasm, and with a face that so clearly expresses the contrary, that one cannot but laugh at Marion, who, despite expressing timid doubts, has the will to believe at any cost. For beneath a certain level of art the person who permits herself to be deceived is as responsible as the swindler. Marion's delusion continues when she confesses to Pauline that she knows that Henri loves her less than she does him but more than he is yet willing to confess and that she will make him fall deeper and deeper in love with her. Note that this scene occurs after Henri had sex with Louisette and the latter has already confessed it to Pierre (with whom she tries to get a date, too, but in vain, given his fixation on Marion).

Pierre is less delusional than Marion, but Rohmer pokes fun at him, too. His love for Marion is honest, his outrage at Henri not simply based on jealousy but on his aversion to seeing people work at their own unhappiness, as is often the case in erotic affairs. Unfortunately, however, he is himself one of those unlucky fellows, for he undoes any chance that he might have with Marion by behaving toward her in a way reminiscent of hers when dealing with Henri. Both are possessive and jealous, and neither has the patience to wait until the other side slowly gets erotically attracted. They both hurt themselves by talking too much, as the initial verse suggests. Pauline, who recommended Pierre to Marion and prefers him by far to Henri, still tells him that he has no mystery for Marion, who knows him by heart. Marion herself declares to Pierre that he is too similar to her (indeed, both Sylvain and Louisette think the two are siblings); she needs someone who complements her and about whom she can dream. (Analogously, Henri will explain to Pauline that Marion's physical perfection oppresses him and that she did not leave him time to desire her.) Pierre lacks empathy, sees love mainly as a rational affair, and refuses to acknowledge the element of folly that, even according to Pauline, belongs to love. He even dreams of revenge: when Marion will finally love him, he will have fallen out of love. Pierre, who always insists on equilibrium while teaching the two cousins windsurfing, lacks the sense for the equilibrium needed in an erotic relationship.

His possessive attitude extends to Pauline, too, who rightly tells him that she is not his ward. It is not clear how serious the erotic intentions are that Pierre develops with regard to Pauline. For in order to have her peace, Marion has encouraged him to aim at Pauline, whom she also tries to convince to become the much older Pierre's girlfriend—in flagrant violation of her responsibility for her charge. But Pauline is not interested in elder males, and she has no reason to become a surrogate for another. She sincerely likes Sylvain, even if she immediately feels that he is sexually more attracted to Marion than to her and dislikes his bet that Marion will become Henri's and not Pierre's lover. That for a short time she imitates in a more innocent way the relationship model that the grown-ups act out before her is more than natural. What is so endearing about Pauline is not simply the intelligence of her observations; she grasps both the chemistry and the morality of love much better than the adults, despite, or in truth because of, her limited experiences. What makes her the true heroine of the film, even, as we will see, a redeeming figure, is her basic goodness. The cordial way she takes leave from the paternalizing Pierre is touching, and after she has warded off Henri, who approaches her with obvious intentions, while she is asleep in his house, with the most elegant kick of film history, she is sincerely worried that she might have hurt him. But her kindest gesture comes when the two cousins leave the beach house, earlier than planned. Marion avows that the suspicion has arisen in her that it was not Sylvain but Henri who was with Louisette; and while she still does not believe it, she generously invites Pauline to think that this was truly the case so that she might overcome her disappointment with Sylvain. The cordiality with which Pauline accepts her condescending offer without a hint at the true state of affairs, which has been

Image 9 Pauline (played by Amanda Langlet) waking up after Henri's sexual advances

disclosed during Marion's short absence, reminds us of François's silence at the end of the first story and of Jean-Louis's discretion. It is a sign of true affection; and we hope that this girl, who tries to love her fellow human beings and see positive things in other persons while not letting herself be fooled, will experience more happiness in her erotic life than the people half a generation older.

One Woman, Three Men, and Three Forms of Love: *Les Nuits de la pleine lune*

Les Nuits de la pleine lune (*Full Moon in Paris*) of 1984 again unfolds three forms of love; but it is now one and the same person who feels all three of them in relation to three different people, no longer the unhappy triangle of *Pauline* "A loves B, B loves C, and C loves someone else or is unable to love," which leaves everybody unsatisfied. Louise's first type of love is semi-spousal, for she lives together with Rémi, who loves her with all his heart. Precisely this is the problem: for Louise loves less if someone loves her too much, and she does not want to make her lover too happy. Rémi tells her that if she reciprocated his love to the same extent, they would already be married—"and divorced," as she adds. Already the acting of the first scene displays how tense their relationship is, mainly because their lifestyles and interests are utterly different. Louise, who does not yet want children, because she does not feel adult enough, furthermore reserves for herself the right to leave Rémi if she finds someone whom she likes more; and she wants to enter into a contract with him that he will not make a fuss about it when she informs him. (The category of rights is symptomatic of how she, and most people of her generation, understands a relationship.) Despite his love, he understands that this contract is too much to her advantage; and after she ironically declares that at least he then has the guarantee that she likes him more than others, she concedes that he has the same right to leave her—even if she hastens to tenderly remark that in such a case she would suffer a lot and then covers him with kisses so that the contract cannot be discussed further. Her second relationship is with Octave, an intellectual friend, with whom she loves to hang out, even if she is not erotically attracted to him but only likes him as a friend, albeit she is more flattered than annoyed by his desire for her as a woman. Third, she is herself sexually captivated by Bastien, with whom she passes the last night of the story in her private Paris apartment, which she insists on keeping beside the larger apartment shared with Rémi in the suburbs—even if the initial proverb warns us that having two wives and two houses leads to the loss of soul and reason respectively. While the French aristocrats of the eighteenth century kept their petite maison for affairs in the countryside, Louise has it in the middle of Paris; and at the beginning she claims, deceiving herself as much as her interlocutors, to need it in order to enjoy solitude. But her unfaithfulness with Bastien leaves her completely unsatisfied, and while she justifies it by declaring to an unknown person in a cafe that she engaged in it because she did not want to love Rémi only out of pity, she now feels that she is truly at home only in the suburbs with him. But when she returns, he is not there; and when he arrives, he tells her that also he was unfaithful this night of the full moon, with Marianne, a friend of her friend, with whom he has decided to stay for good. The gentleness with which he informs her shows that there is no revenge involved; he simply was no longer willing and able to live in this precarious relationship and is sure that he will be happier with Marianne. He took Louise at her word.[6]

The name "Marianne" helps us to recognize that Rohmer is offering a remake of Renoir's *La règle du jeu*, which, as I already mentioned, is based on Musset's *Les caprices de Marianne*. The rare name Octave occurs in both Renoir and Musset, and Rohmer's Octave has an analogous position to the heroine, who in all three dramas is torn between three men (Musset's Marianne between her husband Claudio, the passionate lover Coelio, and his friend Octave; Renoir's Christine between her husband Robert, her former lover, the aviator André, and the common friend Octave). In all three cases, the sense of commitment and ownership that inevitably goes hand in hand with a marriage, erotic passion, and amicable feelings are the three main facets of love, distributed to three characters, and the husband/partner ultimately triumphs (either by subjecting his wife or, as in Rohmer, replacing his partner by another). None of the three heroines is able to integrate the three facets of love into one relationship, and this leads in the case of Musset and Renoir to the death of the passionate lover, murdered deliberately at Claudio's behest, erroneously killed by a jealous servant who confuses Christine with his own wife in Renoir's film. In Rohmer's film nobody dies, for none of his love stories is tragic. This has partly to do with the evaporation of the honor code of the aristocratic society, which forms the basis of both Musset's and Renoir's works. The husband in the latter's film, Robert, is the Marquis de la Cheyniest. Rémi, on the other hand, is an administrator of a modern suburb, who lives there himself because he regards this as more honest; his gymnastics and tennis playing have replaced the hunting activities of the high bourgeoisie and aristocracy so sarcastically mocked by Renoir at the eve of the Second World War. The daring aviator André has become the saxophonist Bastien, who no longer has a passion for one woman but likes to sleep around. The feasts the partier Louise attends may be a functional equivalent of the celebrations of Renoir's heroes, but they are transposed into a much lower social and cultural key.

Only Rohmer's Octave, brilliantly played by Fabrice Luchini, has a certain formal greatness: he is an intellectual, who detests nature and can only live in the center of the country that is the center of the world, namely Paris, pursues his pretentious activities in anonymous cafes, throws around words like "ingenious" and "sublime" to name utter banalities, declares that he likes to seduce for seduction's sake, because only this allows him to feel still young, and at the same time shows contempt for individual differences since the eternal feminine erases all individuality. He is rhetorically more sophisticated than Henri, and has to be so, since Louise has no reason to throw herself at him, still having a partner and feeling no physical attraction for Octave, who is far less muscular than Henri. His seduction efforts are comparable to those of Chloe, even if the seducer is now a man, as befits the inversion of the gender axis that occurs in the *Comédies et proverbes*. In his movements as well as in his arguments, Octave is something of a serpent. Despite having a wife and a child, for whom Louise fakes concern, he courts Louise with enormous stubbornness, being probably really jealous of both Rémi and Bastien but certainly acting his jealousy in a way that cannot fail to impress Louise, whose purportedly virginal and Amazon-like spirit he lionizes with the most barefaced impudence. Louise speaks with him more about herself than with the other two men, a fact that demonstrates that her relationship with Rémi is in shambles; she even talks with Octave about Rémi, regarding whom Octave suggests that Louise chose him, although infinitely inferior to her, because unconsciously she is afraid of any rejection and therefore does not aim higher. She is not wrong to betray him, but not with a person who is even lower, such as Bastien, while he, Octave, is a much better alternative. When Louise bluntly confesses to him that he does not attract her, he corrects her that he does not attract her bestially, like other men do. Not all of what he says is wrong, such as when he corrects Louise and avers that giving away herself sexually does not concern such a small part of the self, since sex engages the whole person. The trouble that he takes with her at the end pays off, for after Rémi has announced her split, Louise calls Octave and invites him to visit her that evening in her Paris apartment. He will be more obliging than Musset's Octave. Her rush into the next entanglement reminds us of Sabine; no woman

Image 10 Octave (played by Fabrice Luchini) courts Louise (played by Pascale Ogier).

takes the time to pause and reflect. Also formally the ending of the fourth comedy is parallel to that of the second: for in both films, beginning and end correspond to each other, since *Les Nuits* both starts and ends with Louise calling Octave.[7] He will get her, at least for a few nights, and Louise's last words, a triple "sure," are in strident contrast to the emotional chaos to which her desire for formal liberty condemns her.

The Search for the Confirming Sign: *Le Rayon vert*

Le Rayon vert (*The Green Ray/Summer*) of 1986 offers, like the last film of the cycle, at least the hope of a happy ending, but while in the later film this is the result of complex emotional shifts and some machinations, the happy conclusion of the earlier film is due completely to chance. This, perhaps, is the reason why Rohmer refrained from writing an explicit screenplay and entrusted the incarnation of his story to the gift of improvisation of his actors, particularly the lead character.[8] The dialogue of this film is therefore inevitably the least literary of all sixteen films. Shot in 16 mm, the film relies partly on amateur actors. The title of the movie is reminiscent of a novel by Jules Verne, and while the reference to Musset and Renoir in the former film does not occur within the filmic universe itself (it is thus a case of discreet intertextuality), Verne's novel is explicitly discussed in the film, as will be Shakespeare's romance in the last of the films dealt with in this book: in both cases, we may speak of explicit intertextuality.[9] Delphine, the heroine of the film, is, like the sea mammal that her name evokes, an exception in the world in which she lives. When we hear that the heroine of Verne's novel is like a fairytale character, such as Cinderella, we inevitably think of Delphine herself.

She is the only round character of the film, which is, as no other film by Rohmer, fundamentally a psychological study of an individual person; even her potential partner at the end remains sketchy. Neither flirtatious, like Anne and Louise, nor calculating, like Sabine, Delphine is a romantic; but unlike Marion, she lacks the vitality and the self-deception that vitality often enough requires. Pure and at the same time fearful of men to an almost pathological degree, Delphine was three times in love, is now single, but has difficulties accepting that it is over with her ex-boyfriend; she longs for a new partner, but she is neither willing nor able to engage in the flirtatious procedures that may open up the chances for a partnership. She is a convinced vegetarian, somehow disgusted by the vulgarity and brutality of life. She feels her loneliness particularly when the long summer vacations approach, even more so since a girlfriend has just rescinded her plan to spend the vacation with her.

No doubt, the torment of what to do with one's vacation is a luxury problem: the grandfather of Delphine's friend tells her that he only late in his life got vacations, that as a Parisian he likes to stay in the capital, and that for him the Seine replaces the sea. But even if a luxury problem, it remains painful for Delphine, whose fragility Marie Rivière, who also had acted the very different character of Anne, captures extremely well: when alone, she often cries; she is afraid of contacts with persons whom she does not know; when speaking, she rarely terminates her sentences. Delphine lacks the erotic urge that characterizes her girlfriends—Manuela gets excited even when she moves her hands along the statue of a naked man. Delphine's friends are all more or less benevolent, but their benevolence consists in wanting to transform Delphine into one of them. Béatrice—whose name means "the one who makes happy" and ironically reminds us of the female heroine of Dante's *Commedia*—suffers from the helper complex; even though she hardly knows Delphine, she tells her bluntly that she, Delphine, is sad and that she, Béatrice, is there to help her. She immediately goes over to insinuations about Delphine's childhood and declares that she, Béatrice, is aggressive only in her friends' best interest. Delphine's repeated asseverations that she is fine are patently contradicted by the way in which she utters them; and the fact that she is the center of condescending attention does not help to lift her morale either. When she reproaches Béatrice for always speaking, the latter responds that this is so because she has more to say; and Delphine rightly objects that one may have things to express even without expressing them. Indeed, Delphine is richer in her personality and in her emotions than the people who surround her; but since they are the majority, they are convinced that they are the norm and exert a relentless pressure on her to adapt. When one friend brings her to Cherbourg, to spend some time with her own family, even her little niece asks Delphine about her boyfriend, whom she does not have; and the necessity to make one up as well as the feeling of not fitting within this completely normal and well-functioning family explain her departure. Having returned to Paris, she is permitted by her ex to go to his place in the Alps. The contrast between the sublime majesty of the mountains and her solitude, increased by the memories of the end of her partnership, is terrifying, for her as well as for the audience, and she leaves the same day that she arrived. When she meets another friend in Paris, the latter offers her an apartment in Biarritz for the rest of her vacation. Her lonely roamings there are interrupted when she meets a Scandinavian tourist, Léna, who in a cafe explains to her that she likes to play with men to whom one should never show what one has in one's hands. The personality contrast between the two women is highlighted by the camera: Delphine is filmed in front of the sea, which stands for loneliness and nature, Léna in front of vacation apartments, a symbol for artificial sociality. When Léna begins a flirtation with two young men in the pidgin French and pidgin English that so often forms the basis of intercultural vacation sex, Delphine flees from the futility of impending physical intimacy without emotional commitment. But when she waits for her train back to Paris the next day she is approached by a young man, who is intrigued by her reading Dostoyevsky's *Idiot*. The magic of falling in love, alluded to by Rimbaud's verse at the beginning, finally takes place.

Delphine's forlornness has indeed something in common with Prince Myshkin's. But fate has kinder intentions concerning her. That she finally meets a man whom she likes and who is sincerely attracted to her as a person is either chance or an act of grace, certainly not the result of her own effort, which Delphine rejects, nor an outcome of the various beatific social activities of her well-meaning friends. But how can Delphine know that this time her trust is justified? How can she have true insight into her prospective partner's and into her own sentiments (for one's own feelings may be deceiving as well)? The story presents Delphine, unlike Françoise, not at all as a Catholic. Still, with deep anthropological acumen, Rohmer shows us throughout the film how much Delphine relies on external hints about her fate. Whether they have objective meaning or, like the prodigies of ancient times, only serve the psychological function of reassuring a person who lacks the confidence to make an independent decision Rohmer leaves artfully open; probably he thinks that the need for signs is human but that in this reliance on something that transcends oneself something divine manifests itself. Horoscopes, posters, and the playing cards that she picks up on the streets are all hints for her; and the final clue is the green ray that appears at the end and about the role of which in Verne's story she overheard a conversation of tourists. Note, however, the enormous difference from Verne's 1882 novel. In it, Helena Campbell declares that she can only marry after having witnessed a green ray merely because she wants to avoid the threat

Image 11 The loneliness of Delphine (played by Marie Rivière)

of a marriage with a man whom she does not love; and when finally the rare phenomenon occurs, she does not see it, because she is busy kissing the beloved she has encountered in the meanwhile. Delphine is more traditional than Helena—she says "yes" to spending some days with her new acquaintance only after she has seen the green ray, asking him to wait until it appears. This is not, she explains to him, because the sign brings luck but because it warrants trust. In a world in which all sentiments are so easily counterfeited, for Delphine, the warrant of trust can only come from outside.

Elective Affinities in an Erotic Quadrilateral: *L'Ami de mon amie*

L'Ami de mon amie (*My Girlfriend's Boyfriend/Boyfriends and Girlfriends*) of 1987 also ends with the formation of a couple, in fact even of two, although we have reason to presume that only one will last. But while chance plays a role, its role is minor; we observe the dynamic between the four people involved for a long time before the new coupling occurs. Since A and B are a couple at the beginning and C hopes to gain D, the final pairing of A and C, on the one hand, and B and D, on the other, has something in common with what in chemistry is called a double replacement reaction, as Johann Wolfgang Goethe's famous novel *Wahlverwandtschaften* (*Elective Affinities*) suggests.[10] The difference, however, is that in Rohmer's movie C and D are never a couple outside of C's phantasy and that also A and B are not married; thus the recombination of partnerships lacks the tragic dimension it has in Goethe's novel. For the failure of the promise given in marriage is always tragic, and perhaps even more so when it is no longer perceived as such. Our film, however, is ultimately cheerful, thus rather reminiscent of William Shakespeare's *A Midsummer Night's Dream*, which starts with the structure A (Helena) loves B (Demetrius), B loves C (Hermia), and C loves D (Lysander) and where the involvement of the fairies is needed to bring about a solution, or of its filmic transformation, Ingmar Bergman's admirable *Sommarnattens leende* (*Smiles of a Summer Night*), where even four new happy couples are formed out of ailing relationships. But while the Protestant Bergman perhaps attaches less importance to the dissolution of marriage bonds (in truth, however, one marriage in his story has never been consummated, and one estranged married couple reunites), Rohmer, and even more his favorite character, Blanche, has much respect even for an amorous bond short of marriage. This explains the somber traits that also characterize this film, although its ending corresponds much more to what a traditional comedy was supposed to unfold than all the other so-called comedies of the cycle, which depict rather failures of relationships or the miraculous stroke of luck that a deeply melancholy character experiences. Comic, no doubt, is the use of the proverb that inspires this film. For "The friends of my friends are my friends" may well be true in a generic way, but given the excluding nature of erotic relationships hardly holds for erotic triangles, which can never end with the satisfaction of all three persons involved and sometimes even leave everybody unhappy or at least unite the third character to a fourth outside the original set. Fortunately, however, the proverb works better for quadrilaterals, as long as we do not have a situation of one woman confronting three men, such as in *Les Nuits*, but the genders are balanced and two men face two women. Rohmer deliberately works with the numbers three and four, as if he were to try all possible combinations; he clearly understands that formal structures impose their own abstract logic on erotic entanglements, as he enjoys playing with formal geometric structures in the images of his films.

Blanche, herself not a beauty, comes as a young administrator from the provinces to the new Parisian suburb of Cergy-Pontoise, whose modern architecture has something theatrical and thus alienating—people move within it as on a stage. There she meets the flamboyant Léa, who introduces her to her boyfriend, Fabien. Blanche teaches Léa swimming and eyes in the pool the beautiful Alexandre, whom she has already remarked on. The two young women speak with him again, when they meet him in a café and where they find out that his relationship to Adrienne is falling apart. Léa then informs Blanche that she has to leave for her vacation, without Fabien and in fact in the company of another young man whom she wants to try out. In her absence, Blanche and Fabien meet by chance, but twice within a short time, since the shopping center in their suburb is relatively small, and the second time Fabien invites her to join him while lake surfing on the weekend. It is after their third date that they fall in love with each other and even spend a night together. But in the morning Blanche tells Fabien that this cannot be continued, partly because she is still aiming at Alexandre but mainly because she feels deeply ashamed at her lack of loyalty toward Léa, to whom she had proclaimed that the boyfriends of her girlfriends are sacred. When Léa returns, she tells Blanche that she is back again with Fabien. But a few days later it is definitely over. When the two women meet again with Alexandre, it is obvious that he lacks any interest in Blanche, who withdraws. Now Alexandre begins to court Léa, even before she tells him that Fabien has been subsumed under the category of the "ex." When he suggests that she move in with him, she demands that he wait at least six months, which Alexandre is able to bargain down to six days; and very shortly afterwards she confesses to him that she has the impression that she has been together with him—not six days, as he hopefully asks, but six months. Also Fabien and Blanche declare their love to each other, but Fabien has to depart. While waiting for him at a restaurant a few days later, Blanche is discovered by Léa, who has come to dine with Alexandre. She goes alone to her to inform her about having conquered the beau Blanche had adored. When she tells her that she is terribly sorry but that "they" fell in each other's arms, Blanche assumes that she refers to Fabien and is deeply distressed. When Léa tells her that she had no right to be loved, she agrees in principle but complains about all that "he" had promised her; they had even slept together. Léa is outraged at Alexandre's presumed unfaithfulness until the two women understand that they were speaking about different men. Still, Léa is amazed that Blanche used Léa's absence so well, and when the two men appear the two women declare that they were wrong to worry for each other; and the two couples take leave, wishing each other good vacations.

The symmetric misunderstanding at the end, based on different references, belongs to classical comedy—think only of the twin comedies from Plautus to Shakespeare. While there the confusion is a result of the physical similarities between identical twins, the bewilderment in Rohmer results from the use of the personal pronouns and the fact that, given the different additional information each of the two women has access to, each has reason to regard it as superfluous to replace the personal pronoun by the explicit proper name. The situation is symmetric also insofar as both Blanche and Léa have conquered their friend's ex or potential boyfriend. The plot of the two deceived deceivers is a classic comic topic; Rohmer uses it in the second episode of the 1995 portmanteau *Les Rendez-vous de Paris* (*Rendezvous in Paris*), where the wife who finally has promised to spend a night with her boyfriend, since her husband has told her he would be out of town, on the way to the hotel sees her husband entering it—with his girlfriend. This is funny, but no more.[11] The symmetry at the end of *L'Ami*, on the other hand, hides deep asymmetries. The apparent one is that only the insecure Blanche believes herself to be the loser. This fits with the character, who shares some traits with Delphine—we see her, too, weep alone, because she proved unable to exploit a chance encounter with Alexandre. But as Delphine finally gets what she longs for, so also Blanche is the true winner, for only she has the right concept of love: Léa was right when she told her that only Blanche was searching for the extraordinary. Another grace of the movie consists in the fact that people do not only misinterpret each other; they misinterpret themselves, too. Very soon, the viewer of the film feels that the relationship between Fabien and Léa is brittle for the simple reason that they are too different (Léa likes presents, surprises, provocations, appearances; Fabien hates them), that Fabien and Blanche respect each other from the start (she has tact; Fabien comments on her after the first quick encounter), and that Léa is erotically profoundly attracted to Alexandre, even if she is too proud to make the first step. When she and Blanche speak the first time about him, she tells her that neither is he her type, nor she his—an ultimately correct but surprising insight, given the fact that she has just begun to come to know Blanche. We are not wrong in surmising that this female intuition is a function of her desire to reserve Alexandre for herself, for she tells Fabien bluntly that Alexandre is superior to him, and her joy when she perceives that Alexandre and Adrienne are splitting is unmistakable. True enough, she pushes Blanche to approach him, but one need not share all tenets of psychoanalysis to recognize in it a projection. When, before leaving for her vacation, she gives Blanche a ticket for the French open, she mentions that she will meet Alexandre there only in her last sentence, after having spoken a long time about her difficult relationship with Fabien and even having laughingly alluded to the possibility of Blanche inheriting him. Léa's later encounters with Alexandre, even if under the pretext of bringing him and Blanche together, are so obviously flirtatious that here, at least, one wonders at her honesty. When Adrienne mentions to Blanche that she has sung her praises to Fabien, her aggressive reaction, analogously, cannot simply be ascribed to her desire to remain loyal to Léa; one feels that Fabien has turned into a real temptation. Needless to say, even if Adrienne, like Léa, sincerely likes Blanche, whose modesty, refusal to appear more than she is, and desire to see the positive sides of other people are truly endearing, she pursues her own agenda; for since Fabien and Alexandre are the two only more or less free men in their environment, by directing Blanche toward Fabien, she may gain a chance to reconquer Alexandre. Analogously, Blanche's hesitation in front of Alexandre is due not only to timidity, but also to a deep desire for Fabien, which she is not yet able to recognize openly. Her tears afterwards are honest, but unconsciously they are also an expression of the fact that her failure with Alexandre has increased the probability of a conflict between her duties as a friend and her needs as a woman, a conflict from which she truly suffers.

Neither Léa nor Adrienne nor Blanche really engage in deliberate machinations, otherwise Léa would not be so surprised at the end, even if one grants that a humiliation is more difficult to perceive than an erotic triumph. What Rohmer depicts so skillfully is rather how erotic attractions are determining our behavior, and even our talk, long before they are allowed to fully penetrate the stream of consciousness. There exist unconscious machinations.

Blanche takes her obligations as a friend so seriously because love, for her, is also a form of friendship. When Fabien tells her about his increasing difficulties with Léa and that a person like Blanche immediately seemed more familiar to him, she reacts by saying that this is the contrast between friendship and love—in friendship, similarity is more important, whereas eroticism prefers difference. But we soon see that this is not really her conviction—or, since we do not want to reproach her with a lie, that her behavior knows more than her abstract theoretical attitude. For during her third excursion, in that melancholy hour, when the sun prepares to set, walking from the bank of the Oise toward an abandoned park, Blanche expresses her irresistible feeling of ease with Fabien, even if she wishes that she might be as happy with the one whom she still believes herself to love, Alexandre, as she is with Fabien, whom she still regards only as a friend. But after this confession, the first physical contact follows naturally, and sexual intimacy ensues when Fabien makes it clear that no revenge against Léa is involved and that he feels as if Blanche and he were the only people on earth. This emotion is already articulated in the *Iliad* (16.97ff.), and it is an adolescent but characteristic way of conceiving the duality and totality of eroticism. The whole scene is probably the most romantic one in all sixteen films; the light, the landscape, the silences, the glances, the hesitant and tender gestures, the dialogue, everything contributes to an alluringly lyrical depiction of falling in love, so brutally contrasting with the flirtation of Léa

Image 12 After the double displacement reaction: Fabien (played by Éric Viellard), now with Blanche (played by Emmanuelle Chaulet), and Alexandre (played by François-Eric Gendron), now with Léa (played by Sophie Renoir)

and Alexandre, where the art consists in making a pass without having to lose face if one is rejected, because the first step can then be explained away as merely ironic. It is the memory of this magic moment that brings the lovers back after their split the next morning, which duty dictates to Blanche. When the two meet again after the final separation of Léa and Fabien, a separation about which Blanche pretends to have heard only vaguely, they confirm to each other how much they feel at ease with each other. Fabien explains that his sudden return to Léa was a natural reaction to the leave that he had taken from her—for in such a situation one feels a sudden nostalgia for the former partner; and Blanche expounds that in Alexandre she adored not a person but an image. It is the reciprocal knowledge of the other person and the affinity in value attitudes that makes Blanche and Fabien fit so well. Léa and Alexandre, on the other hand, it is not hard to guess, will go separate ways after having satisfied their sexual desire. They are both superficial; but we already saw in *Le Beau mariage* that not all common traits are sufficient for lasting relationships.

4

Contes de quatre saisons

The *Contes de quatre saisons* were produced in the sequence springtime (1990), winter (1992), summer (1996), and autumn (1998), but since Rohmer ordered them according to the usual series of seasons when he published the screenplays,[1] I, too, will begin with spring and end with winter. On the one hand, the four films show us the evolution of the year—the blossoming of the trees in the first tale, vacationing at the sea in the second, vintage in the third, and Christmas time in the fourth. The changes of the light and the dominant colors that occur over the seasons are grasped with great delicacy, and certainly at least the first three films embed humans in the surrounding nature even more than the earlier films did. Her majestic power is perceived as a healing contrast to human intrigues and wiles. On the other hand, the reduced number of the films—four instead of six—permits Rohmer an even more artful interweaving of the stories. They do not share any common character but mirror each other even more than the films of the two earlier cycles. Thus, the topic of the matchmaker, which had already emerged in earlier films, becomes predominant in the first and the third tales, with the important difference that what is a deliberate machination in the third tale is more the result of unconscious desire in the first. Even the second tale has elements of matchmaking, but here the main topic is an erotic quadrilateral like in *Les caprices de Marianne* and in *Les Nuits,* that is, in the gender proportion 1:3, not 2:2 (as in the last comedy). However, here it is a man who has to choose among three women, while the fourth tale returns to a woman facing three men. More important than the gender inversion is the difference that the second tale displays the refusal of any commitment, while the fourth hinges on the absoluteness of a choice. While the first and third tales, on the one hand, and second and fourth, on the other, belong together concerning their topic, the first and second tales have in common that they do not exhibit the formation of any new couple, while the third does and the fourth repristinates a relationship that seemed irrevocably lost. The presence of two philosophers, a female and a male one respectively, as well as the geographical setting unite the first and fourth tales, which both unfold to a large part in Paris, while second and third tales take place in the provinces. (In the third there is a philosopher, too, but he plays a minor role.) Is there something common to all four films? Yes, they all share some form of erotic renunciation—a topic of old age, dear also to Goethe's last novel, *Wilhelm Meisters Wanderjahre, oder Die Entsagenden* (*Wilhelm Meister's Journeyman Years, or the Renunciants*). Friendship becomes even more important than earlier, sometimes between two women, sometimes growing out of a renunciation.

Playing the Pander for One's Father? *Conte de printemps*

Conte de printemps (*A Tale of Springtime*) deals with the friendship of a philosophy teacher at a lycée, Jeanne, with a young conservatory student, Natacha, whom she meets at a party and who invites her to stay for some days in her apartment, since Jeanne offered her own to a cousin and does not feel at ease in her boyfriend's, Mathieu's, abode when he is absent. We will never see him while Jeanne will meet Natacha's divorced father Igor and his girlfriend Eve, be initiated into the complexities of Natacha's broken family, visit their country house, and almost pass a night there alone with the womanizer Igor. But she departs in time and reproaches Natacha for having tried to pair her off with her father to get rid of the hated Eve; Natacha will vehemently reject the insinuation, but since Jeanne by chance finds a valuable collar that was missing and that Natacha wrongly suspected Eve had stolen, the two friends reconcile. This, in few words, is the action of the film. It seems much less exciting than the earlier ones, since neither the emergence nor the falling apart of a love is depicted. (It is possible that Igor and Eve will split, but we do not see it, and neither Igor's allusions, which further his cause with Jeanne, nor Natacha's wishful thinking at the end settle the point.) The only erotic movement is Igor's courting of Jeanne and its failure. But what distinguishes it from the situation of the *Contes moraux* is the lack of any form of deliberate seduction on the side of Jeanne. In all six *Contes*, one woman actively tempts the man—the exception being, of course, Claire, who leaves that to Laura. Jeanne is a Claire fifteen years older, sober, determined, and bound by a mature love to Mathieu, the strength of which is even more manifested by his absence. She speaks little about him, and when Natacha takes this as a lack of enthusiasm, Jeanne wisely answers that she prefers to keep her enthusiasm for herself. (We have seen how speaking about one's beloved with other people, even good friends, usually indicates some fissures in the relationship.) Jeanne refuses to reflect on whether she would be attracted to Igor, if she were not committed; for she does not love "ifs" and the concomitant dreams. When Igor tells her that she does not seem to be "madly" in love with Mathieu, her reaction is that she would never be madly in love with anyone, for the simple reason that she is not mad. What irritates her most about her situation is that she is married without being married—on both sides, there is absolute commitment, but they have not yet been able to formalize and institutionalize it, and this is, she claims, what in old times was called living in disorder. Since we do not see Mathieu or even witness a single telephone call between the couple, there is no direct way to find out whether Jeanne is faithful on principle or rather because of love, while Claire's love for Gilles was evident from the first moment in which he appeared. No doubt, Jeanne is a principled person, but we do have some evidence of her love. When Jeanne leaves Mathieu's flat at the beginning of the film (after the initial scene when we see her coming out of her school, to which she has the same sense of dedication as to Mathieu), we might think that she wants to leave him; but it is this apartment to which she returns at the end, bringing into it the flowers her cousin left her in her own domicile. To Igor she explains that she did not like to stay in Mathieu's apartment because of its disorder, which she can endure only when he himself is there; and Igor rightly infers that this is a sign of love.

Igor's interest in Jeanne gets started when he meets her while returning to Natacha's flat (he usually lives with Eve) and Jeanne comes out from the shower enveloped in a towel. But the true fascination starts during a common dinner of all four, when Jeanne unwillingly trumps Eve on all accounts. Eve quickly moves from the V to the T form; Jeanne follows suit with some hesitation. Eve is proud of her activities in organizing expositions and communicating with the press and disdains to share her own philosophy, which she mentions alongside that of Plato and Spinoza; Jeanne proves to be an extremely committed teacher, who wants to teach her students true philosophy, not the trendy stuff from psychoanalysis or the social sciences, and learn herself from the pupils. But what is true philosophy? Metaphysics? Jeanne identifies it rather with transcendental philosophy, and while both Kant and Husserl are mentioned, she insists that it is a method, to be detached from individual names. When in her first encounter with Natacha she declared that she loved to think about her thinking, she already pointed in the direction of transcendental philosophy. Is it exaggerated if we see Rohmer's movies themselves, with their refusal of actionism and their focus on dialogue and the inner thought processes of the characters, as a filmic equivalent of transcendentalism? But even more enticing than what she says is Jeanne's absolute seriousness, while Eve only drops names, humiliates Natacha for confusing "transcendent" and "transcendental," and at the same time proves unable to name even one synthetic proposition a priori. The enjoyment the non-philosophical viewer draws from the scene is that he quickly understands that the philosophical dispute is in truth a struggle for Igor, whom Eve fears to lose and Natacha hopes to entangle with Jeanne. But Jeanne herself does not perceive this subcutaneous aspect of the discussion, and this infuses her, who is not beautiful in any traditional sense, with a radiance, which proves even more captivating for Igor. Even the seduction scene proper, in the country house, after Eve has returned to Paris after a quarrel with Natacha, who later left with her boyfriend, is so peculiar because Jeanne does not seem, or at least want, to perceive Igor's intentions. When she declares that it is comforting to speak with him without any background of seduction, she is not flirting. Igor, however, manages to find a transition to his ends by remarking how comforting Jeanne is for him, while all other women have stressed him out and he would so need a sober love. Almost in a trancelike state, she permits him to approach her (later she will explain this as the desire to prove the absurdity of Natacha's plan), but after the third concession (the number being explicitly connected with Hegel) she stops him and even leaves for Paris, when he lies to Eve, who calls him to know whether Jeanne is still with him. Igor confesses to Jeanne that he was not in love with her and only liked to be in love; he wanted to regain the feeling of desiring and being desired that his passionate affair with Eve had extinguished.

Did Natacha really want to pander to her father? This is the real mystery of the film. Natacha probably does not lie when she explains on the next morning that she forgot to tell Jeanne about her father's announced visit; she might have convinced herself that her father would not come to the country house, even if he had so promised (people, after all, do not always keep promises, and she claims to be able to read between the lines); her quarrel with Eve was understandable on its own, even if it had the additional benefit of driving her away; and she is probably honest that she had to leave with her boyfriend, who is the age of her father, for unforeseen reasons. Still, all her actions led closer and closer to the seduction scene. Even when Natacha invites Jeanne, whom she meets for the first time, it is not easy to determine whether she immediately likes her as a person, so different from her, the emotional musician, or whether she sees in her a potential companion for her beloved father, perhaps a surrogate for

Image 13 Confrontation between Jeanne (played by Anne Teyssèdre) and Natacha (played by Florence Darel) caused by Eve (played by Éloïse Bennett), with Igor (played by Hugues Quester) in the background

her mother, whom she misses and despises. But what the final reconciliation of the two women suggests is that the question cannot be answered. Willing occurs on various levels, unconscious and deliberate ones, and it is natural that one sees in a person whom one likes a possible companion for one's mismatched father or that one begins to like a person whom one considers fitting for him. The human heart is an abyss, and even a rationalist such as Jeanne can appreciate this.

One Man, Three Women, and Three Forms of Love: *Conte d'été*

Conte d'été (*A Tale of Summer*) centers around a young student of mathematics with musical talent, Gaspard, who spends his summer vacations in Dinard in Brittany in a friend's apartment, hoping that Léna, with whom he is "sort of" in love, may show up. He meets in a restaurant the elder anthropology student Margot, who works there as a waitress and waits for her boyfriend, who is in Polynesia, to return sometime. The two engage in many walks and talks—for Gaspard the first time that he has a (non-erotic) friendship with a woman, who becomes his counselor in erotic matters. While she rejects his timid attempts at her, she teaches him that Léna, who does not even bother to write him, is not the right choice and suggests for his temporary attention Solène, who has observed him with approval and desire when they were together in a disco. The two indeed get together, which does not seem to please Margot after all, and Gaspard's problems are compounded when Léna finally appears. At their second meeting, however, she is far from gracious, and so he promises to accompany Solène to Ushant, when a phone call by Léna informs him that she is now ready to go there with him. Having two dates at the same time, poor Gaspard is in a true dilemma, from which he is saved when he gets a call that he can buy an excellent tape recorder for a good price if he immediately leaves for La Rochelle. With this godsent excuse he manages to flee from both women, while Margot accompanies him to the boat, rejecting his offer to go, sometime later, with her to Ushant, since she has just received a letter from her boyfriend, who will return, earlier than expected, in September.

The film is one of Rohmer's most hilarious and a brilliant persiflage of the vague and open relationships characteristic of so many contemporary erotic relations. On the one hand, it continues the topic of *Les Nuits*, of a person attracted to three different people of the opposite gender. Gaspard is *interested* in Léna (passion, as he confesses to Margot, is not involved) because of her academic brilliance; her character, however, is one of the most repulsive ones in Rohmer's cosmos of women. After having returned from a vacation with some other young men, who bored her with all their ulterior motives, she treats Gaspard with utter condescendence: "You are better when far away than when close" is probably even meant as a sincere compliment, for this woman completely lacks empathy. She explains to him that she does not have any intention to sacrifice even the least portion of her freedom to anyone—or only to the one whom she will love when she finds him. She already twice believed herself to be in love but deceived herself; and she does not want to make the same error again. When she begins to sob (the only feminine trait that this egomaniac careerist possesses) and Gaspard tries to console her, she pushes him away and runs from him. Solène is no intellectual, but one can understand why Gaspard is attracted to her. To Margot he gives two reasons: first, he wanted to take his revenge against Léna; and, second, he got *interested* in her on her own account. Solène sings well and truly appreciates Gaspard's composition, she is good-looking, and her erotic nonchalance is somehow impressive. The way she picks him up on the beach, wants to know what his exact relation to Margot is (when he tells her that she is not his girlfriend because they met only last week she objects that the two things do not contradict each other), and informs him about having dumped one of her two boyfriends last week and the other today could seem to justify Margot's judgment that this girl is vulgar. But one should not underrate her: she has her principles, one of which being that she never has sex the same day that she meets a man (Marion could learn from it); and the other that she does not play the double game and does not tolerate anyone playing it with her. Since this principle seems to contradict her earlier account of the two boyfriends, she insists that only one was the true *mec*, while she tried only vaguely to replace him with the other. When Gaspard mentions that he had also contemplated going to Ushant with Margot, since she is only a friend, the irate Solène utters one profound sentence, something Léna does not even come close to: friendship is something serious, perhaps something even more serious than love. Of course, this shows that she does not consider love a form of friendship.

This points to the third reason for Gaspard's dalliance with her. It is not only a rest from his unreciprocated courtly love for the haughty Léna, who is much too busy with herself to love anyone else; it is also the right way to get Margot jealous. Again, it is not clear whether he deliberately sets out with this purpose in mind or whether an inner instinct drives him; but no doubt Margot does get jealous. A physical struggle between the two even ensues, an obvious compensation for sexual contact, a release of sexual tension disguised as wrath, like Margot's kiss shortly afterwards that pretended to be a bite. Margot is particularly furious that Gaspard does not admit his responsibility but excuses himself by noting that it was Margot who had alerted him to Solène. His lack of true desire, which hides itself under self-fulfilling pessimism, must disturb her for the reason that it shows to her that this young man is simply not ready to choose, for only then could she have had a chance. Still, the bond between the two is strong and enticing. Léna was for Gaspard's mind, Solène for his body, even if due to her admirable first principle they did not engage in more than some making out, during which we can identify in him a bit of lust, but mainly curiosity, no love, not even passion. Margot is for Gaspard's soul. She is the only woman for whom he develops friendship, but partly his immaturity, partly her status as a woman committed to someone else explain why their interactions do not go beyond some kisses. The grace of the movie consists in the fact that we witness the slow emergence of true affection between these two young people, who, in fact, while speaking about their love affairs with other people, come emotionally closer to each other than to anyone else. Margot may well declare that for Gaspard she is only the substitute of a substitute (a fear Solène will share later), but in truth Gaspard's two other infatuations seem only to occur to give him and Margot stuff to talk about. Their talks on love and friendship are among the best in Rohmer's oeuvre: erotic involvements oblige one to play comedy and to pretend to be another person in order to make oneself interesting; neither with Léna nor Solène does Gaspard feel like himself—while Gaspard and Margot feel as much at ease with each other as Blanche and Fabien. Gaspard is as rationalistic as Jeanne; he, too, dislikes the "ifs" and the *amour fou*. But unlike Jeanne, he is not committed or willing to commit himself. Also, Margot is not yet sure about her boyfriend—she loves him, she confesses to Gaspard, but does not yet know him enough, and according to her predecessor Pauline this means that she cannot yet love him truly either. At the beginning, Margot has pity for Gaspard, whose intellectuality seems to her a serious handicap in dealing with women. For he can only succeed if he really believes in something, and his permanent self-reflection on whether he loves Léna paralyzes him. She guides him with a certain maternal instinct but becomes more and more aware that his pretended weakness is in fact an asset, which various women find attractive—herself included. That at the end the timid boy and erotic underdog has the choice between three women amuses her. She compares him to a clochard who wakes up a millionaire—clearly an allusion to Rohmer's first and unsuccessful feature film, *Le signe du lion* (*The sign of the lion*).[2] Summing up her evolving views of him, she tells him that he seemed to her first an unhappy lover, then an unskillful seducer, then quite sly, then a rascal, and finally not really bad but still very sly. That she has thought so much about him demonstrates that she likes him; and discovering ever new hidden dimensions must have increased the erotic attraction.

Why do Gaspard and Margot not become a couple? Even more than her jealousy her deep insight into his character proves Margot's love: Gaspard is simply not yet ready for the commitment of love

Image 14 Friends or lovers? Gaspard (played by Melvil Poupaud) and Margot (played by Amanda Langlet)

and does not want to make a choice yet. He belongs, she predicts, to those men who become better with age, and he confides to her that a graphologist once told him that only around thirty would he mature. Margot, who feels the urge to become a mother, cannot wait for him, but her sadness at the end demonstrates that, if there was not this lack of synchrony in their development, she would have loved to replace her absent friend by Gaspard. For the two are soulmates; neither will forget their common promenades. Margot's last service to Gaspard is to alert him to the fact that he should not complain about not having been able to conquer any girl—for avoiding that was exactly what he aimed at, with no less instinctive security than Natacha in the earlier tale at bringing Jeanne and her father together. And one has to recognize that Rohmer has brilliantly grasped a new type of male, who is the opposite of macho, whose melancholy complaints about his lack of virility are a powerful seduction strategy, and who, when this strategy becomes successful, indicates that his complaints are correct by fleeing from any serious engagement into music, mathematics, or whatever attracts him more than the stress of a daily relationship with a woman. It is plausible to surmise that Gaspard, like Bertrand, got some of his features from the young Rohmer, who also needed much time before he found his vocation and married.

Playing the Pander for One's Friend: *Conte d'automne*

Conte d'automne (*A Tale of Autumn*) depicts two attempts to find a partner for a widowed winemaker, Magali, initiated by her old friend Isabelle and by the sort of girlfriend of her son Léo, Rosine (whose name reminds us of Beaumarchais's famous dramas). While Magali confesses to long for a new partner now that her two children have moved out, her isolated life does not connect her easily with other people, and she rejects the use of dating advertisements. Without her knowledge, Isabelle publishes a brilliant ad and meets several times with Gérald, telling him only the third time that she is not the woman who seeks a partner. She invites him to her daughter's wedding, where Magali will be too, whom she has chosen for him. The problem is that at the same party Rosine brings Magali together with Etienne, her old philosophy teacher who was for some time her lover and still declares himself to be in love with her. She wants to kill two birds with one stone: by matching Magali and Etienne, she hopes both to do a service for Magali and to be able to maintain an amiable relation with Etienne, who, so she claims, continues to desire Rosine only so long as he is not coupled with another woman. But Magali and Etienne, both of whom Rosine had informed in advance of her plan, do not develop any interest in each other. Magali, however, is attracted to Gérald until she discovers Isabelle in a private room of her house embracing him in order to congratulate him on his success. She is shocked and concludes that they must be lovers, since otherwise Isabelle, who always speaks about finding a partner for her, would have introduced him to her; and her suspicion increases when Rosine tells her that she recently saw by chance the unknown man together with Isabelle. When Gérald drives Magali home she lectures him on the quality of Isabelle's marriage, which one should not endanger (another act of moralizing inspired by jealousy); and when Gérald's answers to her questions become more and more elusive, she suddenly understands the situation and asks him rudely to drop her at a railway station. She returns furiously to Isabelle, who confesses to her the plot; and while she sobs that she has lost through her behavior the chance of finding the right man, Gérald returns too. Seeing the two friends together, he suspects that he has been the object of a practical joke; but Isabelle manages to save the situation, and Magali invites Gérald for the *Fête de la Reboule* at the end of the grape harvest.

Since, unlike the first two tales, the film ends not only with a wedding but with the probability of a further matrimonial knot being tied, it qualifies as a comedy in the traditional sense, and its various intrigues contribute to this classification as well. It ends with a similarly optimistic vein as *L'Ami*; but the difference is that this is the only film in our corpus where the couple that is hopefully formed consists of two elder persons. True enough, there are various films that depict the desire of an older man for a younger woman, such as Jérôme's flirtation with Claire, Igor's pass at Jeanne, the love story between Etienne and Rosine, and Maxence's relation to Félicie in the last film of the cycle; but, being deeply asymmetric, these relationships do not last. Just so, the affair between the equally mature Marion and Henri does not endure more than a few days. The wedding celebrated at the end is not that of the heroes but it kindles some hope for the institution, as does Isabelle's stable relationship with her husband, probably facilitated by them living not in Paris but in the peaceful Rhône region, whose natural and architectonic beauty the film captures with much love. Stability, however, is not without temptation, and the charm of the film consists in demonstrating in detail how the passion for matchmaking is often a sophisticated way of satisfying one's own, not the other person's, erotic ambitions rather than an exercise in charity. For Isabelle clearly enjoys her flirtation with Gérald and the fact that he is increasingly attracted to her, even if he senses that there is something phony in their meetings, since she eludes many questions natural in such a situation. In the scene at her house, before Magali surprises them, Isabelle openly avows to Gérald that she would like all men to love her; and we did not need her confession to know it. Her excitement when she meets him for the first time is composed of erotic tension—including at least the perception of being desired, if not her own desire—and the awareness of the theatrical role that she is playing, walking around in the restaurant until the stunned Gérald approaches her, who, based on her ad, had expected a farmer and thus another type of woman. (We have learned from Gaspard that playing a role and eroticism often go hand in hand, for the unveiling of the body and the soul can only occur after some covering.) Isabelle needs a break from her routine and some play of her imagination; she works, after all, in a bookshop, while the prosaic Magali gains her living directly from nature, which, as she states, she does not exploit but honor. There is something of a pre-established harmony between Magali and Gérald, who is himself the son of winemakers and like Magali was born in North Africa; they truly fit together. But erotic attraction may rather be directed toward those with whom one does not fit, and one of the claims of the last conversation between Gérald and Isabelle before she tells him the truth is the one already quoted above that the issue of type loses importance when one gets older: now one may develop interest in a very different type of person. In fact, however, Magali corresponds to Gérald's earlier wives much more than Isabelle; but that does not prevent his fascination by the latter, for whom he might well have settled if she had not limited her role to that of an ambassador at her own risk or, as Gérald calls her, a good angel. Fortunately, however, he is quite similar to Isabelle's husband, and Isabelle claims to have learnt that the men most different from him are more dangerous to her. Still, her melancholy expression while dancing with her husband at the end proves that there was temptation also for her. She resisted it but she felt it.

Rosine's matchmaking attempt, on the other hand, fails for two reasons. First of all, there is no surprise element involved, while Isabelle tells Gérald that she will organize his first meeting with Magali as if by chance. We know that for Rohmer chance plays a

Image 15 Isabelle (played by Marie Rivière) meets Gérald (played by Alain Libolt) for the first time

decisive role in erotic matters—a chance that can be interpreted as the sudden appearance of grace. For love belongs to the many things in life that cannot be willed as such—they have to be accepted as gifts, like our own life itself. Now, Isabelle's angelic mediation is such an unexpected gift, doubtless for Magali, but in a certain sense for Gérald, too. For even if he comes to the wedding with the intention of meeting Magali, the picture that Isabelle shows him before that is a complete surprise to him. True enough, he is irritated when he finds out about Isabelle's joke on him, and Magali gets furious when she begins to suspect the truth. But not only is their reaction natural, for nobody likes to be manipulated: even if the intent is benevolent, our autonomy is violated, and it takes some time to weigh that violation against the benefits achieved. Magali's wrath somehow mirrors Gérald's anger; and the fact that they both return to the source of their troubles, Isabelle, proves that they are kindred in spirit—as does the fact that both tell Isabelle separately that they find each other possible, and even very possible. Rosine, however, has informed in advance both sides, and even Léo, of her plan, and all three have found the idea unpalatable that Etienne may end up as the step-father-in-law of his former lover, even if Rosine tells Léo that her plan indicates that she is no longer in love with Etienne. Her acting, however, tells us only one thing: she is not in love with Léo, who, as his mother admits, is five years less mature than his girlfriend. She truly likes Magali, but one can hardly marry a person only because of his mother. Why does Rosine behave as counterproductively as she does? One may name lack of experience; Isabelle is doubtless a more consummate woman. But the ultimate answer is that Rosine does not want to lose Etienne. We have seen that Isabelle herself gets more interested in Gérald than she ought to; and Rosine has already been in love with Etienne, and she is not yet out of it. The first scene between the two makes it obvious: she rejects Etienne's physical approaches, but in such a flirtatious and occasionally yielding manner that one feels that she would be even more hurt if he did not try. She pretends to want to have a clear line drawn between friendship and love, while he apprises her that their relationship will always keep this ambiguous. And contrary to what Rosine tells him, Etienne loves ambivalence only in the extras of life, not in its solid part (he deliberately does not call it "profound," since both parts are). When Rosine declares that he must choose between being a courageous seducer of pupils or settling for a wife, she provokes the question whether she would love him to tell her that he will love her for all his life. Her answer is an angry no, but this can easily be explained by the fact that asking her whether she would love him to tell her "A" is not exactly the same thing as telling her "A." She leaves with the threat that they will only meet again if he has found a wife but after less than two weeks she visits him with her proposal. After its failure, she drives home with him, and not with Léo. No word or gesture indicates whether the failed proposal will motivate the narcissistic Etienne to use the right words with Rosine, and even in that case, it is far from clear whether Rosine would accept a marriage proposal, for she is undecided about her life. The only thing that we can say is that her story with Etienne is not finished; it may be over but it is not yet laid to rest. As long as this is the case, she won't be able to bind herself to another man but will probably look for other occasions of merry matchmaking.

Waiting Beyond Rational Hope: *Conte d'hiver*

Conte d'hiver (*A Winter's Tale/A Tale of Winter*) is not the most successful but the most ambitious film of the cycle, for it vies with a daunting model. The title of the film appears in the film, not referring to itself but to William Shakespeare's *The Winter's Tale*, of which we see the final scene represented in theater—the only example of metatheater in the cycles. Shakespeare's play is one of his three romances (or of his four romances, if one counts *Pericles, Prince of Tyre* as authentic, which it probably is only in the second part); like *Cymbeline* and *The Tempest*, it depicts an apparently tragic story, which, however, at the end finds a surprising, harmonious solution. Neither a tragedy nor a comedy, the romance ought to be counted as a third subgenre of drama.[3] Rohmer's heroine, Félicie, calls herself the "unfindable daughter," not yet knowing that Perdita, the "lost one," is the name of Leontes' daughter in Shakespeare's play. But in fact, she corresponds rather to Leontes, for it is through her fault that she is separated from her beloved, like Leontes from Hermione, even though she keeps her daughter, while Leontes temporarily loses Perdita, too.[4]

The wordless quick initial scenes of the film show us a happy love story during a vacation in Brittany between Félicie and Charles, at whose end the woman gives her address to her lover (he did not give his, for he is a cook who lives from job to job in the USA). But, alas, Félicie through a lapsus has mentioned the wrong suburb, and five years later she has not been able to trace him again, although having become a mother by Charles of Élise. For she rejects abortion, not for religious reasons but because it is against nature. She is now torn between two men—her employer, Maxence, for whom she works as a haircutter, and the Catholic philosopher Loïc. She decides to break off with Loïc and follows Maxence to Nevers, where he has opened a new hair salon; but while the first excursion with him alone uplifted her, when she moves there with Élise on Christmas day, she stays only two days and returns to Paris. She calls on Loïc, but she tells him that their relationship can only be amicable, which he reluctantly accepts. He goes out with her to see Shakespeare's drama, which strongly resonates with Félicie, and visits over the following days with her and Élise a small town in the neighborhood of Paris, when Félicie, herself not a churchgoer, sees a church and asks him to enter and pray for her, that is, for what she would pray herself for—which is meeting Charles again, who has remained the only person whom she really loves. Loïc obliges, engaging in a petitionary prayer, which Rohmer approves of because it is not self-centered. When on the last day of the year Félicie rides home in the subway with Élise, her daughter, to whom she had always shown the picture of her father, looks intensely at a man, who returns her glances and then perceives her mother. Needless to say, it is Charles, and while Félicie first rushes out from the subway, because she sees him with a woman, he follows her and explains that this is only an acquaintance and that he had in the last five years only two relationships, which failed (exactly like Félicie's). They go together to Félicie's mother and plan for their common future.

Image 16 A modern anagnorisis: Charles (Frédéric van den Driessche), accompanied by Dora (played by Marie Rivière), recognizes Félicie (played by Charlotte Véry) in the subway

While the final reunion of the loving couple, particularly the inclusion of a child, usually absent from Rohmer, reminds us of Shakespeare, an obvious difference is the *petite bourgeoisie* to which Rohmer transposes the story—from royals to a cook and a hairdresser. Leontes' jealousy does not have an equivalent either, but it is tempting to interpret Félicie's otherwise inexplicable lapsus as an expression of the unconscious desire to give depth to her otherwise too simple love story, which grows through the challenge. What makes Félicie one of Rohmer's most intriguing heroines is her intermediate position between the normal behavior of her generation and the uniqueness of her commitment to Charles. When at the end she tells Charles that she left one boyfriend two weeks ago and the other one week ago, we inevitably think of Solène; but when she adds that she did it for Charles' sake, we feel the difference between comedy and romance. Torn between three men, Félicie seems a female equivalent of Gaspard; but while he fled from choice, Félicie makes an absolute decision in favor of an improbable event, namely, that she will find Charles again and that Charles did not interpret the false address she gave him as a way to get rid of him. As an instinctive philosopher, who without any formal education can express deep thoughts, she declares that finding Charles would be such a magnificent event that this offsets its low probability; and that she wants to live with this hope, for even if it is not fulfilled, it is worth living with it. Her existential wager reminds us of Vidal, but the difference between the two is that she asks for Loïc's prayer. We see furthermore Félicie enter a church in Nevers with Élise; it is there that she decides to leave Maxence. The crucial reason is that she feels that she does not love him enough (she only wanted to love him, and that is not the same thing); but there is also the fact that he too does not truly love her or her child. Even in the first scene, she reproaches him for not trusting her, and the way he introduces her to his employees in Nevers shows that he sees her almost as his property. But why does she move to Nevers? One of the reasons is that she wants to give Loïc a chance to find a woman who can love him as strongly as he loves Félicie (her sister Amélie tells her bluntly that her choice is not so much for Maxence as against Loïc); the other is that she wants to lower the probability of meeting Charles to zero. For the continuous looking out for him—displayed in one of the first scenes when she runs after a man, in whom she wrongly thinks she recognizes Charles, through the masses and the traffic of Paris—tires her out. But in the church in Nevers she suddenly comprehends that waiting is what she wants and ought to do.

    Why does Félicie prefer Maxence to Loïc, whom she really likes as a friend, who loves her, and who is also caring to Élise? In a conversation with her mother, who strongly supports Loïc, she simply states that he is not her type. There are two reasons why she is unable to reciprocate his love: he is too intellectual, and this creates an asymmetry which she cannot endure, especially because she experiences his knowledge as merely bookish, while Charles learnt from life. Sarcastically she will tell Loïc later that if she confessed to him that she loved him, he would look up where in Shakespeare this is written. And, secondly, she wants to be dominated, but physically, not mentally, and Loïc's softness, obvious, for example, in the way he tries to grab after her and immediately yields to any resistance, leaves her sexually unsatisfied. When the mother says that gentle males are rare, she objects "Less than you think," correctly describing an epochal change in masculinity. We have seen in Gaspard's case that this change can become an erotic asset—but with the Margots, not the Félicies of this world. Loïc accepts this rejection not simply as something one has no alternative to enduring; he renounces Félicie by praying for what will make his loss of her irrevocable. The camera respects his privacy in prayer, for it does not follow him to mass, as it did with Jean-Louis; but, albeit hesitant, the prayer must have been sincere, for Loïc truly loves Félicie's happiness more than his own. He thinks that God owes her special love because of the suffering that she has endured, and he deeply admires her not only for her uncanny philosophical insights but because of her transparency: even without a green ray he knows that he can read her heart. Rohmer spends much time depicting Loïc's brand of Catholicism, almost as much as he did depicting Jean-Louis's. In the discussion with friends who believe in metempsychosis, Loïc proves to be as rationalistic as possible: he not only rejects the unchristian idea of multiple lives because it deprives humans of responsibility, he also avows not to believe in the miracles of Christianity, and rejects all assumptions about the supranatural as a form of magic, not of religion. It is not difficult to identify his worldview as some form of ethicotheology in the sense of Kant, even if he adapts to it the traditional forms of the religion of his family. His interpretation of

Catholicism is similar to the one that he ascribes to Plato concerning the pagan religion.

How does Rohmer himself stand to this brand of Catholicism? On the one hand, there is no doubt that he admires Loïc: his renunciation is the purest of the cycle—Jeanne has Mathieu; Margot's boyfriend will soon return; Isabelle has a husband, Gérald the chance to get Magali, so the interruption of their flirtation with each other is not really painful. But Loïc has nobody else; when he goes to his parents, he is the only single one among his siblings, and given his love for Félicie, he will probably remain it. There is true greatness in his prayer, as there is in his capacity to recognize the extraordinary value of Félicie, particularly since she is so different from him. It is, on the other hand, equally obvious that Rohmer appreciates her no less. Félicie does not argue but has an immediate encounter with truth in the church in Nevers; she knows that this is a personal experience that Maxence can never understand. She refuses to call what happened to her in the church a prayer; it was rather a reflection or meditation. She also rejects Loïc's comparison of this with a conversion, and rightly so; for as Loïc says, she does not need a conversion—she is already in touch with the divine. She has sympathy for the doctrine of reincarnation, for it would explain her feeling of always having known Charles when they met for the first time; and when Loïc timidly suggests that she might have known him, too, in an earlier life, she agrees, but then he must have been her brother. (One thinks of Goethe's famous 1776 poem "Warum gabst du uns die tiefen Blicke?"/ "Why did you give us the deep glances?") After the visit of Shakespeare's drama, Félicie avers that it is faith that revived Hermione and then claims that she is more religious than Loïc. One can agree with that, even if she does not attend mass and has no interest in traditional theology; for her commitment to Charles is absolute, and it thus touches upon religion. But religiosity is more than the acceptance of unconditional moral principles, it is the trust that the world is ultimately a manifestation of goodness. Loïc is less religious, for although he respects Félicie's love for Charles, he cannot share her trust that she will find him again. This would be a miracle, and he does not believe in miracles. (Perhaps this makes it easier for him to pray for the fulfillment of her wish since he does not truly believe that it will be granted.) One might compare Loïc with the knight of resignation in Kierkegaard's *Frygt og Bæven* (*Fear and Trembling*), while Félicie would correspond to his knight of faith. The story proves Loïc wrong, and Félicie right. Still, the lack of grandeur with which the story ends, so unlike Shakespeare's, shows two things, one with, one against Rohmer. First: if miracles happen, they do occur in the normal course of events, not by violating the laws of nature. Not even exceptional optical phenomena, such as green rays, are necessary to match the right people (in this case, for the second time); grace that hides as chance can lurk in the subway traffic of a metropolis. Second, however, the ending suffers considerably from Charles' insignificance. The viewer cannot help asking whether the new couple's life will not lack the lustre of the conversation between the hairdresser and the philosopher. Loïc's heroic and sublime self-sacrifice in his prayer, which is utterly altruistic, as eros never is, and Félicie's ultimate trust that all will work out are two legitimate attitudes in which the connection to the divine manifests itself. Should these two complementary attitudes not have been matched in reciprocal love? That this does not occur and that Loïc does not even get the chance to react to the reunion of the parents diminish the conciliatory force of this romance, for the greatest reconciliation is that of opposites.

5

The Idea of a Realist Cinema

The focus put in this book on the erotic constellations of Rohmer's films and on the words of his characters is due partly, no doubt, to my own limits. A philosopher works with concepts, which are inevitably expressed in words, not with images, and so when viewing films he tends to emphasize the verbal part in the dialogue and the logical structure of the plot. But, first, this and the next chapter will investigate also the non-verbal part of the films, which is indeed crucial to interpret them correctly. Second, there are few filmmakers in dealing with whom the focus on dialogues is as natural as in the case of Rohmer. For he began his career as a novelist, and the first erotic cycle is based on six novellas that he wrote without yet thinking of making films of them. It was the failure to find a publisher that motivated him, who had gained a name as a film critic, to transform the medium in which he narrates his tales. After the fiasco of his first feature film, he lacked ideas for new film topics, and suddenly he realized that he could use the unpublished novellas.[1] This decision was facilitated by the fact that the novellas were not really ready. As the success of the movies proves, it was not the story or the psychology of the characters that did not stand scrutiny: the novellas lacked the linguistic finish that gives a literary work its "completeness."[2] Since every literary text, and every film as well, inevitably leaves certain states of affairs undetermined that belong to the world depicted by the artwork, it is not easy to explain when the density of description is reached that makes a story convincing. But one can agree that this density can be achieved either by the means of words or of images. One can describe the clothes of a figure in a novel, or one can present them in a film (with even more determinations if it is made not in black and white but in color). Because of his beginnings as a writer, Rohmer has achieved quite an extraordinary balance between word and image. Already in one of his earliest essays, "Pour un cinéma parlant" of 1948, he complained about the absence of "talking cinema."[3] He asked for the establishment of a new relationship between visual elements and speech, and while not denying that silent film had found a specific filmic language as rich and supple as the spoken one, he declared it necessary to regain more space for speech and dialogue in film—a task rendered possible by the disappearance of the ghost of filmed theater.

While the idea that film is nothing more than the fixation of a theater representation completely misses the specifically filmic works of the camera and the editing, which deeply impact the type of acting too, one ought not to deny that the inclusion of spoken language in film has enriched it, even if in one aspect it has made it more similar to the theater.[4] Why is the transition to sound films an aesthetic gain? It did not appear so to all contemporaries, and at least some thought that sound film was a new art form, quite different in its aesthetic nature from silent film.[5] While it is not wrong that new aesthetic principles became necessary, the transition was not simply a reaction to new technical possibilities but a fulfillment of potentialities contained in the richest concept of cinema. To make this clear, some reflections on the nature of film become inevitable. No doubt, the historical origin of cinema is in a visual art, in photography, that peculiar art that is so much more reproductive of external reality than all the other arts.[6] Its claim to being an art is grounded in the choice of its object, the angle under and the light in which it is approached etc.—choices that do not necessarily express only the artist's subjectivity because, paradoxically, the loss of one dimension in the transformation to a bi-dimensional image can render new traits and even the "essence" of an object better visible. But it is nevertheless true that the "objectivity" of photography is a slap in the face of aesthetic theories that ascribe aesthetic value only to human creations. For the aesthetic success of photography, and insofar as it relies on photography also of cinema, cannot be explained without assuming that there is beauty in nature (including humans), even if art adds a second beauty by its representation of the primordial natural beauty.[7] Cinema is the photographic image not of a state but of a movement. This is not yet a sufficient definition, for if I hold the celluloid in my hands and scroll my eyes over it, I do *perceive that* they depict a movement but I do not *perceive the movement itself*. Even if they tell me the story of a movement, the pictures remain discrete. The possibility of a passage from the perception of discrete stages of the movement to a perception of movement as such, from the perception of images to that of a process of "imaging," is due to the phi phenomena and the fact that there are subjective time quanta: humans can perceive hardly more than ten discrete stages per second, and afterimages persist for a twenty-fifth of a second. This is an anthropological limit, not necessarily shared by other minds and even less necessarily constitutive of physical reality, whose temporal structure may be discrete (with very different mathematical equations needed for describing discrete and continuous time). When twenty-four frames per second are moved before an observer, the spectator thus has the feeling of perceiving a continuously unfolding movement and ignores the black spaces that separate the frames. The first films by the Lumière brothers,[8] still free from editing, simply depict real movements, this being possible either by fixing the camera in front of moving objects and persons or by moving the camera itself. Also in the first case the choice of the right point of view is a creative achievement, so that even there a film is more than a mere reproduction of reality; and since in the second case there is a whole series of changing points of view, the subjective act becomes even more important. Despite the ineludibility of choice, however, film in these two forms is documentary (and thus an irreplaceable source for history). This does not prevent it from possibly having a high aesthetic value, for which fictionality is not a necessary presupposition, as literary masterpieces in historiography or even the sciences prove—think of Gibbon and Darwin.[9] But a film as early as the Lumières' *L'Arroseur Arrosé* (*The Sprinkled Sprinkler*) reproduces a staged episode of forty-nine seconds, and thus the fictional element enters film early on. Still, one could say that the event filmed, the sprinkling, really took place, even if the emotions of the actors must have been very different from those of the characters played—the latter are angry, the former must have amused themselves. A further step is achieved when not only the mental states but also the physical events in the world referred to by the film and those in the slice of the world that is filmed diverge— when, for example, a film character dies, while the actor happily survives.[10] It becomes inevitable in such a situation to develop an ontology of the world created by the film, which has to be sharply distinguished, first, from both the objects, persons, and events filmed and, second, their images that we find on the cellulose nitrate or acetate films.[11] (Nothing prevents films and images from appearing also among the objects filmed and the objects of the world created by the film, but their ontological status is in these cases different from the images that depict them.) Both the filmed objects and their images belong to the *real world*, the former being only *tools* in the creation of the artwork, while the images constitute the real side of the artwork. On the other hand, the fictional universe to which the film refers, or better which it creates by referring to it, is a possible world. To speak precisely about it, we need a semantics of possible worlds, such as that developed in the second half of the twentieth century. The possible world constituted by the artwork emerges for us only thanks to the artwork as a physical object within the real world, that is, the moving images on the film, like the meaning of a word is evoked by its sound. But it still belongs to a different realm[12]—even if in some of these possible worlds, unlike in the actual one, transitions between the real and the fictional world may occur, such as in Woody Allen's *The Purple Rose of Cairo*. Note that the possible world created by a film is never identical with the one created by a literary work, even if the former aims at being the most faithful rendition of the latter (as, for example, Rohmer's *Die Marquise von O...*); for the film will have to settle certain properties, such as the hair color or the type of clothes of the characters, that do not belong to the universe of the novel. Note furthermore that while the origin of film in photography[13] makes it inevitable that the film represents parts of our actual world—be it clouds and waves or concrete cities and landscapes—the objects in the world created by the film cannot be *identical* with the objects filmed; for it is not true of the actual Paris that the concrete erotic entanglement narrated in *L'Amour l'après-midi* happened in it. Still, the Paris of the film is enormously *similar* to the actual city, which may permit inferences partly based on premises true of the actual city regarding the story narrated (see below my reflections on Chloe's possible visit to the Louvre).[14]

Even silent film is more than a merely visual art, because, unlike architecture, sculpture, or painting, it depicts temporal changes, like music and literature. But it is not itself temporal—the celluloid is not fleeting like sounds. In its mode of existence, a film is closer to a painting or, given the many people who contribute to its success, a building than to a theater performance; concerning the content that it represents, however, it is more kindred to the latter than the former. A painting may point to a story but it can only represent a stage of it, even if our literary knowledge allows us to integrate it into a broader context—a *Flight to Egypt* reminds us of the persecution by Herod. But this additional knowledge comes from sources outside the individual painting, while the film, like a drama or a novel, is autonomous in the offering of its tale. Thus, even the silent film stands between literature and painting, because it tells a story, even if by the means of pictures.[15] Whoever tells a story does not simply refer to a possible world (which in the case of the documentary film may coincide with sections of the actual one); he inevitably chooses events within this world as relevant to his story, ignoring others, and accesses them in a particular manner. The famous distinction by Ingarden between represented objectivities and schematized aspects holds for all stories, be they narrated by words (with their duality of sound and sense) or by images (where we can also distinguish between optic features, such as form and color, and the reference to objects). But there is an important difference. Images can directly depict only the physical and not the mental world, while our language may describe the stream of consciousness. (Indirectly, however, images that depict not physical objects but, for example, the objects of dreams may capture features of the conscious mind.) Furthermore, our seeing process inevitably sees only one side of an object; we have to go around it to see it completely.[16] Perspectivity is inevitable in the reception of all visual arts, but, unlike architecture and sculpture, painting and drawing involve the loss of one dimension, and thus the artist herself, not only the recipient, has to choose a perspective.

Film shares this loss but it may represent the whole physical body by having the camera move around it, thus somehow restituting the full corporeality denied to the image. Even then, there is always a choice of the shot—of the field size as well as of the placement of the camera. Even more, editing is based on choices—not all events that constitute the story can be narrated. Often this would be tedious: by stressing certain facts over others, a story gets its logic and uncovers connections that may be causal laws or manifestations of a complex moral order. But sometimes even the most relevant states of affairs remain implicit, because making them explicit would render superfluous the inferential work of the audience, which adds intellectual cachet to the aesthetic enjoyment: art is a specific form of indirect communication. No doubt, editing and creating the specific flow of the various shots have also formal aesthetic qualities of their own that are independent of their contribution to the narration of the story: Rohmer compares this quality to music.[17] Still, the success of a silent film ultimately consists in a polyphony of the aesthetic values that we can ascribe to the objects depicted, the specific images of them made by the camera, the combination of the various images and shots in editing, the story that is narrated, and the way it is narrated by means of the earlier elements.[18] The peak of art consists in directing the various traits to one common end—while a merely decorative film may offer beautiful objects or surprising shots, the great film will use these devices to articulate the idea that the film as whole wants to communicate. This idea will be the generating principle of the plot, the characters, the words ascribed to them, the images that we see, and the order in which we see them. The more links between the various elements, the more thoroughly superfluous and unconnected objects and events are eliminated, the more the artwork resembles a complex organism and the better it is. If one dimension is beautiful in itself but has no "co-expressibility" with the other dimensions—to use the famous term of Erwin Panofsky's classic essay of 1934/1947 (1967)—the film loses its organic nature and fails as film.

Since humans have essentially a mental life, no story about humans can ignore their mental attitudes, which become accessible to others usually through language. Silent film solved this problem through a new approach to body language, that is, body movements that have a meaning: the close-up picture allowed perception of the micro-features of facial expression that not only the theater but also the normal interactions between people do not permit us to discern.[19] Body postures, gestures, facial expressions, and eye movements replaced language proper. This was unrealistic; it exaggerated features that in real life play a more limited role. Still, even the body language of the silent film remains an abstraction from real speaking—it is very different both from the body language of dancers and of pantomimes.[20] Beside facial expressions, paradigmatic situations and the usual behavior in them allowed viewers to infer mental states, too. Still, subtitles, deeply disturbing the flow of images, could rarely be dispensed with. The addition of sound made this device to a large amount superfluous (even if Rohmer occasionally uses it, to date the events in his narrative); but that is not its main achievement. The reason why the sound film fulfills the possibilities of cinema is certainly not that the silent films could not describe events of great complexity or even metaphysical topics—Sergei Eisenstein's *Bronenosetz Potyomkin* (*Battleship Potemkin*) or Murnau's *Nosferatu* are powerful counterexamples. The main reason for including the sound is not even the generic fact that sounds are an important part of reality,[21] the perception of which was schooled by sound film, as the camera taught us to see with new attention; indeed, including sounds allows the audience the inference of certain states of affairs, such as the approaching of a person, for which the silent film still needed a different shot. And even if film music that does not originate in the events depicted may intensify the feeling of the rhythm of a story and the emotions that accompany the perception of the action, this addition, while often welcome, is not necessary for the purpose of film, as Rohmer himself shows. No, the main reason why the sound film is such a progress is that in reality human body language is integrated with spoken language. Depicting human interactions abstracting from spoken language does not render justice to human nature, for humans are linguistic beings. (Ignoring their silent actions and interactions and representing only their words, as is usually done in the theater, is of course no less unilateral.) The replacement for speech found by silent film is an extremely artful but still artificial surrogate that does not capture the essence of humans. That is the ultimate reason why silent film, even if it brought forth extraordinary artworks, was so quickly replaced by the talkies and why a return to it is out of the question.[22] Note, however, that the function of language in a film is very different from that in a literary work—at least as long as a voice-over is not involved, which comes closer to the literary narration of a story. The main function of language in a film is not representing but expressing and appealing—since both we and the characters already see what is going on, language is not needed to describe reality; the speech acts by which people express their feelings and appeal to others belong to the reality that the director is presenting through his film as a whole.[23] "Like images, it [sc. speech] is a part of the life I film. What I say, I do not say with words. I do not say it with images either, with all due respect to the partisans of pure cinema, who would speak with images as a deaf-mute does with his hands. After all, I do not say, I show. I show people who move and speak."[24] The necessity of including speech is particularly evident for someone who, like Rohmer, is interested in erotic life. For human courtship displays involve talk: in a flirtation, the non-verbal part of communication is large but it is almost never exclusive; and an erotic passion that is not mediated by the opening of the souls that is possible only through language with all its differentiating power can hardly be called love. Abstract dialogues on love, on the other hand, get easily boring if they do not inspire the interlocutors—the Platonic erotological dialogues already present lovers debating love. In short, dialogue is crucial for the fulfillment of the possibilities of film, and it has to be much more natural than on stage.[25]

Rohmer's preference for talking cinema is rooted in his realist beliefs. His films want to render justice to reality, and talking is a very important part of it. Rohmer shares his realism with the main French film theorist of his youth, his friend André Bazin (1918–58). In his famous essay on Italian Neorealism, the latter started by opposing aestheticism, which dominates German expressionist film, and realism, and wrote: "Since the expressionist heresy came to an end, particularly after the arrival of sound, one may take it that the general trend of cinema has been toward realism. Thus the cinema ... comes ever closer to the novel."[26] Among the features of Neorealism that Bazin mentions, two are of particular relevance for Rohmer's work: the amalgam of lay and professional actors, which entails a rejection of the star system, and the exceptional documentary quality of the films. Even if the social reality of the French young people portrayed by Rohmer is quite different from that of Italians in the immediate aftermath of the Second World War, Rohmer's precision in the description of the mores of his time is not inferior to Roberto Rossellini's.[27] But perhaps even more important is the moral stance toward reality that Bazin attributes to the Neorealists, despite their urge to change and even revolutionize society: "They never forget that the world *is*, quite simply, before it is something to be condemned" (II 21/264). This commitment to realism does not at all alter the result that fictional films deal with a possible world, though the possible worlds chosen by the realist are very similar to the real world—one could even say that they are more real than reality, insofar as they abstract from contingent events and focus on basic patterns and laws of our world, which in it rarely appear in such a pure form.

What Does Realism Mean for Rohmer?

As a film theorist and historian, Rohmer is more generous than Bazin in recognizing the extraordinary aesthetic merits of expressionism, as his book on Murnau attests. But as a director, he follows closely Bazin's aesthetic ideas. (Sometimes he acknowledges that different principles, such as sticking to black and white or the use of extra-diegetic music, have led to great films;[28] sometimes he indicts all deviations from his realistic axioms.) His two main arguments for the superiority of film to the other arts in 1955 were that film is rooted in photography and its objectivity and that the technical complexities of filmmaking made it more difficult for it to detach itself from the strict rules of a craft, as the other arts did, ultimately to their detriment. For the modern arts, except cinema, remain parasitic on their classical predecessors, as our continued interest in the past proves, so alien to earlier epochs of the arts. Film, however, has not lost its classicism and thus its health; and it is paradoxically its modern technology that permits it to recover an equivalent of the Pythagorean harmony of the spheres. Rohmer likes to compare the film director to a demiurge—the figure in Plato's *Timaeus*, who, unlike the God of Christianity, does not engage in a creation out of nothing but works with antecedent matter and looks at pre-existing ideas.[29] At the end of this life, Rohmer was much more doubtful that cinema could escape the fate of the other arts,[30] but at least his own work remained faithful to the principles of his early aesthetics. What does realism mean for him?[31] We can characterize it by the following features. It means, first, that the universes of his films are nomologically possible worlds.[32] Nothing happens in them that is incompatible with the laws that hold in our world; and while this is a reduction of the possibilities of cinema, which has been truly enriched by devils tempting wizards, mirrors the crossing of which leads to the Underworld, knights playing chess with Death, or film characters stepping out from film screens, Rohmer's special branch of realism is not naturalistic. This means that his world is permeated by spiritual forces, suffused with values, and open to the manifestation of the divine. But it is crucial for him that even the workings of grace are such that they fit into reality. Tester contrasts in this sense Krzysztof Kieślowski with Rohmer: unlike the former, Rohmer "is required by his realism to attempt the far more difficult task of blasting out of the empirical the space of a 'now' in which the lurking of God might be glimpsed."[33] Even extraordinary events, compatible with our laws but only rarely occurring, such as those depicted in Werner Herzog's *Fitzcarraldo*, are alien to Rohmer's understanding of realism. He even avoids geniuses and saints. In the three cycles, his characters, while varying considerably in moral stature, are in no exceptional social position. Rohmer is heir to the eighteenth-century bourgeois drama. Two of his characters profess a similarly realistic philosophy of art. "I do not invent but discover," claims Aurora, and Gaspard avers that no musical composition is truly an invention. I am aware of the fact that Rohmer in an important text distances himself from Aurora's statement: he himself does not discover but combines primary elements like a chemist. Thus, he wants the *Contes moraux* compared to symphonic variations of one motif.[34] But this is not at all in contradiction to the profession of realism. What Rohmer explains is that he is not narrating autobiographical anecdotes: none of the six stories "really occurred." But all could have happened in our world, and the artistic achievement consists in the inner coherence of the stories and the unfolding of the same idea in different forms. By exhausting the possibilities of a basic structure, Rohmer believes that he comes close to the main patterns that recur in our world. Just so, chemists come closer to reality when they look, based on theoretical reflections, at possible chemical compounds.

Second, Rohmer strictly reduces in his films the presentation not of phantasies, which we can read off the dreamy faces of some of his characters (for what is eros without phantasies?), but of their contents. What we see is almost always real in the filmic universe, not only in the mind of one of its characters. The only real exception is constituted by Frédéric's omnipotence phantasies in *L'Amour l'après-midi*, where the women subjected to him are even reincarnating the main female characters of the earlier *Contes moraux*, thus obliterating not only the demarcation between the physical and the mental, but also between the various filmic universes. The blurring of the background points to the merely mental status of what we see. But shallow focus in Rohmer is rare; deep focus is the natural expression of his interest in reality as a whole. In general, there is no equivalent, for example, to the dream sequence, created by Salvador Dalí, that Hitchcock integrated into *Spellbound*.[35] Even less would it be compatible with Rohmer's realism to show us images of alternative narrations of the same story, as in Akira Kurosawa's *Rashomon*[36]—the universe created by Rohmer's films is a possible world, but only what is real within this world can be represented in images, not what is merely possible with reference to it. The discussion on the existence of the external world in *Conte d'hiver*, inspired by the beginning page of E. M. Foster's *The Longest Journey*, is characteristic of the futile characters that engage in it; and it speaks for Félicie that she flees from that discussion. Still, Rohmer has found a powerful symbol for the workings of human phantasy. Mirrors are particularly important in *La Collectionneuse*.[37] Why? On the one hand, they highlight Haydée's narcissism, which belongs to the real elements of the story. On the other hand, they suggest that she herself is losing her reality, because Adrien is transforming her from a human being into the mere object of his sexual phantasies. Since she ultimately aims at this, however, this does more to strengthen than to weaken her real presence.

But not only does Rohmer reject the filming of mental events that do not correspond to reality, he avoids also the filming of mental acts that faithfully refer to the past. In other words, third, he spurns flashbacks, which wrongly ascribe the phenomenological qualities of perception to acts of memory.[38] The temporal order in which the images of the film appear thus corresponds to the temporal order of the events narrated;[39] and so Rohmer does not only repudiate filming even partial lies about the past, as in Hitchcock's *Stage Fright*,[40] but also filming truths about the past, such as we see, for example, at the end of Hitchcock's film *Marnie*, even if this childhood experience alone explains what has happened before in the movie. Not that Rohmer shuns final revelations: suffice it to mention *Ma nuit chez Maud*. But it is crucial that the adulterous relation between Françoise and Maud's husband be not shown but inferred. Narrations are important for Rohmer, but only the act of narrating belongs to the film, not what is narrated. The fact that in the first cycle the narration, with the exception of *Le genou*, does not occur within the action depicted but as voice-over is probably a deviation from strict realism and was later discarded by Rohmer (with the only exception of his last film, *Les Amours d'Astrée et de Céladon*). Note also that while there is no strict unity of time in the films of the three cycles, they usually do not stretch over much time—sometimes a few days, sometimes several months. (The epilogue in *Ma nuit* and the prologue in *Conte d'hiver* are exceptions.) There is also no development of independent actions that only incidentally cross—we can thus speak of a unity of action. The continuous flow of time does not prevent various Rohmer films

(*La femme de l'aviateur, Le Beau mariage, Pauline sur la plage, Les Nuits de la pleine lune, Conte de printemps, Conte d'été*) from having a cyclical structure—the end repeats or mirrors the beginning, at least in some respect.[41] This is well in tune with the reality of time, which is both progressive and cyclical, thanks to the repetition of the same rhythms.

Fourth, Rohmer wants to capture not only social reality as it is, but as much as possible nature's beauty, too.[42] While in the first three items discussed he seems to render film similar to theater, only film allows him to represent nature's splendor, brutally reduced in theater to some set constructions.[43] Even a film like Sidney Lumet's *12 Angry Men*, of which 96 percent takes place in a jury room, would be alien to Rohmer's sensibilities: five of our sixteen films play at least partly at the sea, one on a lakefront, another occasionally on a pond on which one can surf; and the films concentrated in the French metropolis, whose architectonic grandeur he pictures with care,[44] usually include scenes outside of it—be it in the banlieue or in a country house, be it in the medieval towns Le Mans or Nevers, with various images of the hectic travel between the two destinations, obviously a symptom of the inner unrest of his characters.[45] (There is definitely no unity of space in his films.) He prefers to shoot outside of buildings, and his sense for the spatial arrangement of a place is always exquisite. While the screen is smaller than a stage, in Rohmer it often represents a larger space than the theater can contain. It is tempting to interpret the third scene in *Les Rendez-vous de Paris* in such a way that it sheds light on Rohmer's work. The hero is a mediocre painter, whose attempt at seducing a woman fails and who at the end in vain waits for a second woman he had kept in the background as a possible replacement. His paintings impress neither of the two women, and rightly so, for they are awful. Under a strong light and in front of a large landscape we see many persons, but none of their faces is individualized. This painter knows how to handle light and space—but he has capitulated while dealing with the human person. This could be a criticism of the modern visual arts, for indeed the genre of portrait does not fare well in our time, and Rohmer bore a particular grudge against Francis Bacon.[46] But it seems plausible that Rohmer wants to suggest that humans, whose characters he himself can draw with few strokes as precisely as few film directors, are indeed often disappointing when compared with the majesty of the surrounding nature, which is not simply a container but almost seems to pass judgment on human folly, be it sea or mountain. Particularly in *Le genou* and *Le rayon vert*, the contrast between the Alps and Jérôme's irresponsible flirtation with Laura on the one hand, and Delphine's utter loneliness on the other is heart-wrenching. Still, the landscapes filmed in *Le genou* are only two, for Rohmer did not like creating postcards and avoided deliberately averting the attention from the characters.[47]

Rohmer's peculiar conception of realism entails, fifth, that he rejected technical tricks—for example, to bring about the green ray at the end of the film with this name; he accepted, however, an image that was brought back from the Canaries, where the story does not play. But at least it was the image of a real event.[48] Already in 1949, in an essay heralding the rise of color film, to which he remained faithful after *Ma nuit chez Maud*, Rohmer wrote: "Film is the most realistic art ... Let the filmmaker work with things and leave their reproduction untouched. We ... demand ... that the image capture the beauty of the world. ... all the world's beauty will never be excessive."[49] Wherever possible, Rohmer relied on natural light; but in order to get the natural light where needed and avoid electrical light, his cameraman, Nector Almendros, used mirrors for *La Collectionneuse*—one of those compromises without which realism cannot produce beautiful films.[50] Rohmer's awe for natural light includes his representing the changes of colors caused by alterations in the illumination by the sun.[51] At the end of *Le Rayon vert*, the appearance of the green color, circumstantially explained by a pedantic German professor in teutonic French, has at the same time a symbolic meaning—it stands for hope.[52] Again, physics and metaphysics do not exclude each other but subsist together. While individual films deal with the change of lighting over the course of a day, the third cycle offers us the rhythm of light and colors over the course of the four seasons—with green particularly strong in the spring, blue and yellow in the summer, red in the fall, and grey in the winter. No less important are the colors of clothes in order to distinguish different personalities in the films—I already mentioned the red Laura and the blue Claire, and something analogous holds of Blanche and Léa in *L'Ami* (Blanche, in honor of her name, sometimes liking white) as well as the three female friends of Gaspard in *Conte d'été*. Rohmer's interest in clothing, as a process crucial for the self-interpretation and presentation of people, particularly when in search for love, is profound. At the end of *L'Ami* the ex-partners, real and potential, wear the same colors (green and blue respectively), while the newly formed couples have different ones, pointing to the fact that what proved finally attractive was a certain complementarity and not superficial similarity. Complete nudities are much rarer than one would expect given the topic, and sex scenes are almost absent (one exception being the short one at the beginning of *Conte d'été*, which helps us to understand Charles' paternity). Even in the beach scenes, what fabric remains to cover the body, be it a tiny bikini, as in the cases of Haydée, Claire, and Pauline, is as important as the body itself. Rohmer takes no interest in the naked male torso, as in Murnau's *Tabu*; Henri's naked breast is presented as repulsive. True, Claire's knee is paraded in the beauty of its form and its colors and as an organic part of her body, but it is the contrast with her clothes that makes it so attractive.

The same respect for nature as it is can be discerned, sixth, in Rohmer's use of sound.[53] He is far from interested in the human voice alone: think of the song of birds, the noise of airplanes, and the barking of dogs in the third prologue of *La Collectionneuse*. The last sound perhaps evokes the ancient Cynics—for those so-called dogs were rumored to practice public sex[54]—while the airplanes remind us that this seemingly idyllic lifestyle is only possible due to modern industrial society and that it mirrors its alienation. Later in the film, we will listen to the chirping of crickets, and in the first episode of *Quatre Aventures de Reinette et Mirabelle* we hear all possible noises of a night in the countryside, until Reinette teaches her friend, and indirectly us, to listen to the absolute silence that can be heard only in the minutes immediately before the dawn.[55] The two friends succeed only on their second try, for the sound of a truck heard from afar destroys the magic atmosphere of stillness. In his book on music, Rohmer quotes with sympathy Kant's famous complaint about the lack of urbanity of music, which imposes itself on the freedom of one's neighbors,[56] and praises him as the first critic of noise pollution.[57] He explains that the main reason why he rejects film music is that music deprives cinema of its peculiar objectivity—its realism. At the same time he recognizes that this objectivity allows cinema—as such, without accompanying music—to transcend the realm of representation and approach the Will, which Schopenhauer taught that only music can express. For Rohmer, cinema unveils the thing-in-itself among the phenomena and allows us to discover the secret song of the world hidden to ordinary perception.[58] While Rohmer generally avoids extra-diegetic music, that is, music that does not originate in the world represented, music is welcome when it does—as with the concert played in *Ma nuit chez Maud*, where realism goes so far that the actor playing the famous Soviet violinist Leonid Kogan is Leonid Kogan himself. But we hear also Gaspard playing his guitar or Pauline and Sylvain dancing to the music of a record they have put on. There are even a few cases of extra-diegetic music—for example, when at the end of *La femme de l'aviateur* we hear Arielle Dombasle (who does not act in this movie but in several others by Rohmer) sing "Paris m'a seduit" (Paris has seduced me) or when the final appearance of the green ray is accompanied by music composed by Jean-Louis Valero.

Regarding acting, I have already mentioned Bazin's remarks on the Neorealists. Like them and like Bresson, Rohmer uses, seventh, both professionals and lay actors.[59] He was always aware that his way of making films, which were often produced at low costs and deliberately reduced energy use, would limit his reception to a relatively small audience; but his desire for ecological behavior and aesthetic autonomy had priority.[60] (Rohmer was usually able to shoot his films in a relatively short time, because much was laid out in advance: for example, he planted himself the rosebush from which Jérôme picks a rose for Laura.)[61] He founded his own production companies, never directed a film not written by himself, and he rejected the star system, partly because few stars permit the other actors to unfold their own potential. No doubt, he had famous actors work for him, such as Jean-Louis Trintignant, Françoise Fabian, or Jean-Claude Brialy, and he helped start the career of various younger actors, such as Fabrice Luchini or Marie Rivière. Some of his actors were uncannily similar to the roles they were playing, such as Zouzou (Danièle Ciarlet), who struggled with drug addiction, to Chloe. But Rohmer has often integrated amateur actors and even complete laypersons—one of the two young men flirting with Delphine and the Scandinavian woman was found in the last minute on the beach of Biarritz; the hosts in Cherbourg were really the relatives of the actress Rosette.[62] He thus offers a broad range of different types of characters; and while as a man he, too, might have had his type, as an artist he integrates the most various plethora of women into his films—there is no preference for blondes, such as in Hitchcock. By reusing his favorite actresses after decades, he managed to enrich their spectrum and avoided nailing them to a specific role.[63] All this fits well with Rohmer's realist beliefs: the world is rich in forms, and there are certain roles that people who naturally correspond to the character desired can represent with ease, without any necessity of acting, which is an art not always required in order to create the character needed.[64] For some people are the characters that actors have to play. Some of the actresses of the most charming figures in Rohmer's films later gave up acting, such as Laurence de Monaghan, who was the perfect Claire, but after a few other roles studied and practiced law. Furthermore, *Le rayon vert* is not alone in coming alive through ad-libbing. Rohmer, while extremely articulate in both the whole composition and the substantial contents of the dialogue, again and again allowed and encouraged improvisation. He even adapted his conception of the film to the peculiarities of the actors he chose.[65] This, too, follows from a realist tenet—for normal human conversation has something unexpected in it. When speaking of dialogue it is crucial to distinguish between what is said and how it is said. Rohmer's literary background made him lay much more stress on the concrete content of his conversations than other directors. But as a film director, he knew that what was said had the appearance of reality only if it came out in a way that fitted with the nature of the character as presented by the actor[66] and built up on non-verbal communication, such as glances and touches, not to speak of involuntary twitches of the face, as in the case of Jérôme when Aurora tells him that one could write good stories even about insignificant people like him. In situations of courtship, Rohmer often exhibits the contrast between what a character says with words and what he or she expresses with body language, partly deliberately, partly because the sexual drive is stronger than his or her conscious will. Particularly in women, a tension between an explicit no and simultaneous gestures asking for the continuation of flirtation is frequent (think of Margot dealing with Gaspard, of Rosine reacting to Etienne): for at least the past created social pressure toward modesty, and the market value of women who yield too quickly falls. But it is not the case that persons only pretend to be repelled while they are attracted; the human soul is such a heap of contradictory forces that they are sincerely both things at the same time. The criticism that Rohmer is a literary director is thus to a large degree unfair. His ambitions for the literary part of his films are high, and this does not hurt them, but they are subordinated to the desire to paint a plausible interaction between persons. That the interactions between his characters are mainly verbal is thoroughly realistic. For while killing occurs, in and outside wars, it is fortunately less normal than falling in love and talking.

In his essay "The Evolution of the Language of Cinema," Bazin contrasts directors who put their faith in images with those who trust in reality.[67] Needless to say, he prefers the latter, and he subsumes the fascination by the montage under the spell of the image.[68] It thus does not come as a surprise that Rohmer, eighth, likes long takes—which oblige the director to take space very seriously. Due to long takes, we read in the Hitchcock book, a director becomes more of an architect than a painter.[69] Rohmer's editing is mostly inconspicuous; the jump cuts so dear to Godard—think only of *À bout de souffle* (*Breathless*)—do not fit with Rohmer's realism (one of various signs that the *Nouvelle Vague* was quite a heterogeneous movement). Rohmer's shots go from rare extreme long shots (he prefers panning shots in order to visualize the connection between characters and landscape), to long, full, and medium shots; since he considers talk the basic mode of humanity, he only rarely uses close-ups. For, first, we have already seen that they originate in silent film, as a surrogate for spoken language. And, second, close-ups focus too much on the individual and less on the relation between characters. But they are appropriate when what Rohmer wants to manifest is an ambivalent emotional state, transparent, if it really is, only to the one who feels it, such as Maud's when narrating the death of her lover or Isabelle's at the end of *Conte d'automne*.[70] Occasionally we find freeze-frame shots or extended shots of an unmoved object made from the same position of the camera, often to symbolize some break in the action; they may focus on objects that also physically signify a barrier, such as gates or staircases. A special function is given to shots where we see certain events through a frame within the filmic universe, like a gate, a window, a mirror. Our view often coincides with that of a character, as when Frédéric views himself in the mirror in Chloe's apartment or Pauline discovers her cousin in bed with Henri through a window going toward the garden. The limitation of the view that a frame can cause explains why some of these pictures are ambivalent: both Pierre and we see only the naked Louisette in Henri's bedroom, not knowing who else is active there. But point of view shots are not frequent, for they contradict the second aspect of realism as discussed above.

Some of the frames allude to classical paintings. We have already observed that Rohmer, truly a *poeta doctus*, often refers, discreetly or explicitly, to literary texts and films of the past. Explicit artworks occur in his films, such as the concert in *Ma nuit*, the theater representation in *Conte d'hiver*, the fresco of the blindfolded Don Quixote on the purported magical horse in *Le genou*, or the reproductions of the paintings that Picasso created in Dinard in Gaspard's room. Similarly, we have discussions on modern painting (Picasso) in *Triple Agent* and on some specific modern industrial architecture, defended by Gérald and, as the images show, also by Rohmer, in *Conte d'automne*. Film within the film is never shown (unlike television), nor are any concrete films mentioned,[71] even if it would fit well with realist assumptions—for modern people love movies. What comes closest to it is the use of the camera in *La Femme*—and it is almost inevitable that one interprets the criticism of voyeurism as a self-criticism and as a criticism of the audience as well, for what, after all, are Rohmer and his aficionados if not voyeurs on a high level (voyeurs not of the sexual act, but of the erotic entanglements)?[72] From the presence of artworks within the possible world constituted by the film, we have to distinguish sharply similarities between the properties of a film and/or individual frames on the one hand, and those of paintings on the other. Such similarities are not in contradiction with realism, for paintings mirror natural reality, too; furthermore, people are influenced in their behavior by their conscious or unconscious memory of iconic paintings, and the director's desire to build on a tradition is a sign of respect toward the past and honors the world more than the claim to begin anew. Concerning the first similarity, Almendros tells us that Rohmer asked him to create a Gauguin look when shooting *Le genou*; not only lighting but also the costumes were adjusted to that aim.[73] Regarding the similarities of individual frames, one example may suffice; two will follow in the next chapter. Needless to say, Rohmer does not try to recreate in a slavish way the original, for what would be the purpose of such an act? (Only in *Die Marquise* did he strive to reenact Johann Heinrich Füssli's *The Nightmare*; but his failure convinced him that one should not aim at an exact reproduction.[74]) What counts is a structural analogy between painting and frame. Note that such analogies are something that in most cases happens to the characters without them being aware of it. A sudden *post festum* realization of such a similarity—"look, we are positioned like the characters in Caravaggio's *The Musicians*"—is possible in principle but rare and would quickly destroy the subsisting similarity, for such an embarrassing insight was alien to the models. We could, however, imagine not only the director but the characters themselves deliberately staging such a similarity, in the manner of a *tableau vivant*. It is tempting to interpret one of the most famous frames in Rohmer in this way—I mean that of the naked Chloe waiting on her bed for Frédéric. Her position is that of Dominique Ingres's *Grande Odalisque*, even if the luxury of the draperies is eliminated in accordance with Chloe's more modest social status; but the bareness of her apartment only heightens the alluring nature of her body, somehow enhanced by her excited face, which stands in stark contrast to the composure of Ingres's concubine. There is reason to believe that not only Rohmer has the painting in mind when positioning Chloe in that way—but that she herself has. After all, the painting hangs in the Louvre, which Chloe must have visited, and it will have struck a chord with her. Needless to say, another aesthetic role of the frame transcends Chloe completely and can only be ascribed to the director—the contrast of her inveigling nudity with the vulnerable nakedness of the pregnant Hélène in the bathroom at the beginning of the film and the fleeting, somehow reckless nudity of the au pair running out from the shower. These cross-references of the images are for the viewers, but it may well be that they are perceived, at least retrospectively, also by Frédéric, whose flight from Chloe is motivated by the sudden insight into the similarity of the image of himself that he sees in the mirror to the one that he remembers.

6

Content and Form in *Pauline à la plage*: Interweaving Words and Images

To show more in detail the interweaving of form and content, of images and words in Rohmer's films, I will now analyze a specific movie, painfully aware that all his films would merit such an in-depth analysis, but which is impossible given the limits of this book. I select *Pauline à la plage*, a film that stands quite in the middle of Rohmer's œuvre and which hides beneath its narrative elegance complex religious allusions. They seem not to have been noted in the literature, and I am quite skeptical that Rohmer ever revealed them to his actors. Would Pauline have eaten her apple so graciously if she had been alerted to what the gesture was pointing to? Inevitably, the film director must manipulate his actors and actresses, even if in a kinder spirit than Henri. While the vanity of an author is flattered when he is the first to discover something, I must declare that I find it stunning that nobody saw the biblical allusions before me, not even an author like Tester (2008), who has the word "theology" in the subtitle of his book. I am aware that we live in a post-Christian age and that, say, a Quentin Tarantino scholar need not be too much informed about Christianity. But when dealing with Christian artists, some of whom still survived into the twenty-first century, it is an imperative hermeneutical maxim to render oneself familiar with basic Christian ideas, however much one may dislike them. For the odds are that they will exert a strong influence on an author's work and shed light on it, perhaps even more than the last turn of the postmodern screw.

Since Rohmer began late to make films, he was already sixty-three when the film was released. But his mind was youthful, and the technical means he used were still those of a beginner. For this masterpiece (which was the fourth of five films by Rohmer to receive the Prix Méliès and was also awarded the Silver Bear for Best Director at the 33rd Berlin International Film Festival) was shot in the course of five weeks, with no assistant director, scriptgirl, set designer, makeup staff, or wardrobe designer. There were only three people for the camera, two for the sound, and no grips.[1] The simplicity of the plot invites us to focus more on the formal features of the film, and the reduced number of characters is helpful, too, particularly since Rohmer chose the ideal actors: the fifteen-year-old Amanda Langlet as the heroine, a girl curious about eroticism, initially trusting in her relationship with her cousin, and transpiring true benevolence toward everybody; Arielle Dombasle as Marion, flirtatious, fearful of the impending loss of her youth, pretentiously romantic, manipulative, and sly ultimately even in dealing with herself; Pascal Greggory as Pierre, a languid *beau* unhappily in love, who in a childlike way feels entitled to the reciprocation of his feelings and does not shy away from telling on his rivals, like a boy in school; Féodor Atkine as Henri, astutely honest, when it increases his sex appeal, otherwise an instinctive liar, mostly avoiding eye contact, with a tattoo on his right arm and a protruding Adam's apple, usually walking barefooted and bare-breasted (somehow anticipating the iconic images of a later Russian president), lecherous, loveless, and with a smile of superiority and contempt for all people who still believe in something beyond hedonism; Simon de La Brosse as Sylvain, a teenager with an earring on his left ear, submissive to his father, in need of a new *ersatz* girlfriend for the summer, after the other broke off their relationship and the real one has remained in Paris, and full of anger at the manipulative grown-ups, whom at the same time he looks up to and wants to hang around with; and finally Rosette (Françoise Quéré) as Louisette, with grotesque bad taste, a pink ribbon and a cheap necklace, always open for beach sex, and nonetheless endowed with pride, for example in her two fiancés, one of whom is even living in America. (One may ignore a friend of Sylvain and Henri's daughter Marie, who say only a few words.)

A formal feature of the composition of the film has already been mentioned—the end mirrors the beginning. The initial frame represents a closed gate, then we hear a car approach, even before we see it, its noise accompanied by the barking of dogs. Pauline gets out of the car, which has stopped in front of the gate, and opens it. At the end of the film, she will close it before she enters the car, dressed exactly as she was the first day (in the meantime, she has put on many different clothes). The gate is not simply an allusion to the beginning and the end of the film: it symbolizes that the unfortunate holiday is an intermission in Marion's life, with nothing to be taken home from it. Pauline's generous silence, however, occurs just after she has closed the gate, and this proves that she at least has learnt something from her vacation—maturity. After getting out of the car, Marion declares herself happy that the neighbors have left and there is no phone in the house,[2] which is surrounded by a beautiful garden—the only other house in which the story unfolds, however, has one, and this will bring the love idyll to an even more abrupt end than one could have expected. We observe the two cousins in the garden, Pauline taking care of the hydrangeas, Marion seated at the garden table and drawing. She is a fashion designer and stands for artfulness, while Pauline's love for the flowers connects her with nature.[3] Pauline for a while is standing and leaning toward the seated Marion—in a gesture of respectful obedience due to an elder relative. When they both sit, the camera captures their four feet that are very close to each other—an anticipation of the interweaving of their arms immediately afterwards and of their adventures not much later. While Marion pretends to desire only rest and declares herself able to stay hours and hours in her house without moving, Pauline confesses to wanting to go to the beach and meet people. It is Marion who astutely moves the conversation to eroticism—does Pauline want to meet boys or girls? The interest that Marion takes in Pauline's up to now quite modest erotic life is obviously not an interest in her as a person; her whole body language betrays that she is getting erotically excited herself and that the condescendence with which she speaks to Pauline is not really rooted in the wisdom of maturity. Her tired and languid glances, her covering her eyes when coquettishly claiming that perhaps she is too old to understand Pauline, are gestures by which she prepares for flirtation; and while all that Pauline says radiates honesty and common sense (for example, the distinction between erotic imagination and really believing something), Marion's final comments that she hardly believes she was already married and that her marriage failed because she never really believed herself married point ahead to the fact that she will soon become the victim of her imagination. For the latter takes over when people are no longer able to believe obvious facts, which, furthermore, ought to be the object of some attention.

The Imagery of Fall and Redemption

The beach, on which the next scene unfolds, is a habitat opposite to the edenic garden, in which the two cousins were sitting. The garden around the house, lovingly attended by Pauline, stands for the union of nature and culture that Rohmer approves, for his ecologism is not of the wild sort: nature can, and ought to, become more beautiful in human custody. The seashore is nature in a more dangerous shape; the threat of drowning is real. The tides of the Atlantic not only cause the splendid reflection of the light, so well captured by Almendros, in the puddles that remain when the sea withdraws; they remind us of the ultimate precariousness of human life, which can be swallowed up by the sea. But even more threatening than nature are the people who hang around on the beach. Fiona Handyside points out the contradictory nature of the two beach images in film culture around 1960: "One stressed the beach as the site for an European art cinema and its interest in realism, modernist narrative ambiguity, and isolated protagonists; the other the beach as a site of mass culture and popular, modern leisure activities, such as sun bathing and wearing skimpy swimming costumes."[4] The first image is found in an iconic manner in the final shots of François Truffaut's *Les quatre cents coups* (*The 400 Blows*); but also Maud's appearance in the dunes and Delphine's lonely walks around Cherbourg evoke it (in *La Collectionneuse*, that image is both called forth and parodied). Still, most beach scenes in *Le rayon vert* and almost all in *Pauline* and *Cote d'été* refer to the second image, which inevitably imposes itself with the spread of mass tourism.[5] Pauline is drying off with a towel her cousin, in the pose almost of a servant, when Marion discovers Pierre. The way she runs to him shows that more than friendship is involved, and, particularly when Pauline interposes herself between Marion and Pierre, Marion's turn so that she may stand closer to Pierre betrays that Marion's erotic imaginations that had begun to flourish in the garden could easily become flesh with Pierre. But now Henri approaches, after having observed the group for a while. From Pierre's deeply irritated face one can read that he immediately understands that Henri will be a formidable rival. When Henri's daughter Marie runs to her father, he takes her up, and her legs around him inevitably are reminiscent of intercourse. Not that there is any suggestion whatsoever of an incestuous relation, but we gain the impression that Henri, probably more in an instinctive than in a deliberate way, instrumentalizes Marie to make himself more interesting with women (after all, he awakens the impression that he is a responsible father); and part of this instrumentalization is the stimulation of unconscious sexual phantasies. Marie's position must have stoked the fire burning in Marion, and she accepts the invitation to dine in Henri's beach villa, although Pierre suggests a restaurant.

The scene in Henri's villa, in fact provided with far more furniture than he claims to own (a model ship points to his inexhaustible need for travel), is extraordinary in its dialogue, which has already been discussed. But no less interesting are the gestures and movements of the characters, due to a masterful *mise-en-scène*. Henri manages relatively quickly to send Marie to bed; he does it with the charm of a person who wants to get rid of another without hurting her. "The time flows by too quickly with you," he says, and she reciprocates. One feels that both lie, but that Henri is much better at it, because he can build on long experience. Originally, Pauline sits behind Henri's back, skimming through a journal, while Marion sits in a chair close to the window, caressing her own left shoulder and moving her hand down the neck, which displays a coral necklace, and Pierre is playing with his hands. The movements are expressions of their erotic tension. Only Henri sits still, able to observe and evaluate the situation with all objectivity, since he is not in love. He plays cat and mouse with his guests. Pauline seems to feel it, for she gets up, moves first to the fireplace (Marion was speaking about the fire with which she wants to burn, but the fireplace is not lit—it will be lit only much later when Louisette visits Henri, who, if he could burn, would burn for her), and then walks over to Marion to sit beside her. The gesture is gracious because it signals both humility and a desire to protect her elder cousin, on whose right knee she puts her hand. Later, Marion will pet Pauline's head, but only after calling everybody, including Pauline, opaque. The gesture is an unconscious attempt to compensate for the rudeness of her words, which fly in the face of good judgment and are mainly signaling to Henri that she does not share Pauline's cautious attitude toward love. All these gestures can be easily explained psychologically. But suddenly Pauline begins to eat an apple. Whence does it come? And why now this appetite? One might answer that she was hungry, for we have not yet seen the cousins eat. But Rohmer's realism is far more complex than that. And indeed it is hard, once one opens up to the possibility of a religious dimension of the film, not to think of the story of the fall in Genesis 3; for Pauline, by observing all the lies of the three adults, is losing her innocence, so charmingly displayed in the first scene in a garden that I already called edenic. Henri is an equivalent of the serpent in Paradise: Pierre will in fact later compare him to a snake, and Marion will demonstrate how she has lost all perception of reality by responding that it is rather she herself whose body has serpentine forms. Henri's deeply irritated reaction to the proposal to drive to Mont Saint-Michel evokes the devil's fear of churches (represented, for example, in Murnau's *Faust*)—a fear particularly appropriate in this specific case, since the archangel Michael was believed to have defeated Satan. Even Henri's slandering of the naïve Sylvain (whose name means "man from the woods") marks his diabolic nature, explicitly ascribed to him by Pierre at the end: for "diabolos" in Greek means "slanderer." Henri even magnanimously pretends to take all sins upon himself—a blasphemous parody of Christ's mission, even if probably not deliberate, for he is not cultivated enough for that. (Even Louisette uses an expression from the Gospel, the language of which, no longer connected to its source, has infiltrated popular use.) Note that these traits are spread all over the story; it requires some attention to connect them and grasp the biblical pattern that Rohmer has in mind. The parallelism with the story of the fall is enhanced by the fact that Pauline's making-out with Sylvain will occur in this same house. The two are encouraged by Henri, who seems to want to keep Pauline busy so that Marion may have more time for him; but he may well want to prepare Pauline for his own purposes, for in his house he will almost rape her. When we look at the latter scene in detail, we shall find out that Rohmer is not only referencing the Old Testament.

The subsequent scene in the nightclub, which, like the later dance scenes at Henri's, are accompanied by music originating in the story itself, offers a sketchy and parodic anticipation of the double replacement reaction that forms the subject of *L'Ami*. For at the beginning Henri dances with Pauline, in whose view of love he had shown considerable interest in the scene in his villa, and Marion with Pierre. Pierre's enthusiasm about having found again the love of his youth, the renewed *coup de foudre*, however, is not reciprocated; while she tolerates some fondling, Marion pushes him back when he kisses her. The falling down of her shoulder strap indicates that this woman is ready for more nudity, but it is not Pierre whom she has chosen. She interrupts the dance between Henri and Pauline and pushes her cousin into Pierre's arms (with the barefaced lie that Pierre wants to dance with her), while beginning to dance passionately with Henri. She then invites him to her house, and as soon as the tired Pauline withdraws, repeating Marie's earlier act, Henri puts his hand on Marion's leg. We already know what will follow, but

Pauline is stunned when, walking into the garden next morning and peeping through a window not completely closed by the shutters, she discovers the naked couple asleep. Her white nightgown contrasts with the pink hydrangeas: it is appropriate to think of a defloration, not, of course, of Marion, but of Pauline, who is losing her mental virginity (and risks losing her physical virginity as well later in the film). Her face expresses sadness rather than condemnation when she discovers what her cousin's discourses ultimately meant.

In the next scene at the beach, when she first meets Sylvain, Pauline is dressed in blue and white, while the sail of the surfboard is red and white—perhaps a compliment to the French Tricolor, the three colors of which we shall later recognize in Sylvain's clothes. Despite having been rejected, Pierre holds Marion with much more passion than Pauline while trying to teach the two women to surf. But Marion leaves him and walks over to Henri's villa. Through the window she sees that he is typing, and like the young girl that she would love to be she climbs through the window to him. After professing her love and getting a quite disappointing answer she moves to another window; sitting on a red towel, expressing the flame she is ablaze with, she forms a splendid contrast to the old trees in the background, whose green symbolizes the quiet wisdom of nature in opposition to human folly. Similarly, the lush vegetation of Marion's garden forms a stark contrast to Pierre and Marion's quarrels in the next scene, when Pierre comes to warn her of Henri. The lies that Marion tells him (even if she confesses that she is fascinated by danger) are mirrored in the disapproving glances of Pauline, who, however, discreetly withdraws, enabling Marion to suggest to Pierre that he court her cousin instead of her. His verbal reaction is negative but his body language demonstrates that he is not completely turned off to the idea. The next beach scene offers the first real flirtation between Pauline and Sylvain, who, as soon as he has eyed her, runs down the stairs taking off his shirt.

While sitting together on the beach and asking about each other's erotic life, Sylvain first puts sand on Pauline's leg, then caresses it, but is pushed back when he tries to grab her. Henri discovers the budding couple with obvious pleasure and invites them to his own house, where they can hear a disk that he has just bought. He leaves them alone, telling them that they can simply pull the door when they leave since there is nothing to steal—though later this too will be shown to be a lie when Marion cannot enter the closed house. The dance of the two teenagers radiates eroticism, enhanced by Pauline's very narrow white bikini that even leaves part of the anal fissure visible. They soon go upstairs to the bedroom where Marion will discover them shortly afterwards and withdraw "under moral shock," without having been noticed by the two young people, too busy with each other. Marion was looking for Henri, whom she will soon meet outside, after he has exchanged some words and glances with Louisette, which show that they are not foreigners to each other. Marion's breasts are very well recognizable, almost palpable under her white shirt, and one sees that she is much more passionate about her Henri than Pauline about Sylvain—Pauline is simply curious and imitative. Henri and Marion first encounter Louisette, whose impertinent glances directed at them slightly worry Marion, and then the teenagers, who, as Henri regrets, did not have enough time to do great things.[6] In the house, the elder couple dance too, and then Henri begins to undress Marion—we see her naked breasts, which were first, if only barely, covered.

Suddenly, the camera turns to Mont Saint-Michel, whither Marion had announced that she and Pauline would drive the next day, and we see from afar the two women driving home in their car, tiny figures compared with the enormous monastery on the hill. The contrast between Marion's breasts and the sublimity of the medieval abbey, underlined by Henri's pretentious remark that the sight of a tourist could bring out the killer in him, is one of the strongest effects of montage in Rohmer, and it is continued when the camera turns to an almost empty stretch of the beach, with Henri and Louisette frolicking with each other in the sea. The message of the montage is clear, while still following the temporal sequence and the logic of the narrative: the collapse of Christianity is the ultimate reason for beach promiscuity, and it is silly to complain under these circumstances if one partner is quickly replaced by another. The couple is joined by the surprised Sylvain, who runs down the staircase to them after catching sight of them. The lonely and somber Pierre, in his black wetsuit and carrying his surfboard, forms a powerful contrast to the group: we see him looking intensely at something, and even if the camera does not do us the favor of showing us the object of his glances, the repulsion that we recognize in his face suffices for drawing the correct inference. The three then go to Henri's villa, where Henri and Louisette withdraw to the upper floor, while Sylvain watches a television documentary about boats. Pierre, a red sweater over his tanned shoulders, passes by the house to find out whether his suspicion is justified and beholds, through the window, the naked Louisette jumping on a bed, but not the other person in the room. When Marion returns earlier than predicted from Mont Saint-Michel to the villa, Sylvain runs upstairs to warn the couple, and Louisette runs into the bathroom, into which Henri thrusts Sylvain, too. When Marion comes up, she sees movements behind the panned bath door, and Henri, later standing in front of a window behind which a tree without leaves symbolizes nature turned barren, is inventive enough to make up that the two had just run from the bed into the bathroom and orders them to leave. The scene in which the two, Louisette covered only by a towel, Sylvain with a naked torso, both humiliated and ashamed, leave the bathroom and walk down the staircase is deeply comic. But one does not have to be very familiar with Christian iconography to recognize in their descent the expulsion of Adam and Eve from paradise, even if the angel driving them out and standing above them is Satan rather than Michael.[7] (My guess is that among the innumerable possible models Rohmer has Masaccio's famous fresco in the Brancacci chapel in Santa Maria del Carmine in Florence in mind.)

The next scene brings Pierre's second visit at Marion's house. When he arrives, the cousins are plucking apples. This reinforces the topic of Eden and the fall and at the same time quotes the cherry tree scene from *Le genou*: when someone is a classic, as Rohmer knew he was, he is permitted to quote both the Bible and himself in one single breath. The conversation between Pierre and Marion, at the beginning sitting in front of each other, with his legs in beige trousers enclosing hers in white ones, tackles again their different concepts of love; when Pierre says that Marion's place is in Paris, not in the Southern Ocean, she remarks that he will soon reproach her for betraying France. Pierre stoops to telling Marion what he has seen—he even would have photographic proof if he had carried a camera. But Marion believes herself to know better: Louisette was with Sylvain. While Pierre shrugs his shoulders, Marion's body language is very similar to that of Louise when dealing with Rémi, namely, half compassionate and condescending toward the unhappy lover, half insecure. She passes her hand over her hair and finally asks Pierre, standing at the other side of his car, which separates the two persons, to drive Pauline to the beach. He understands that she wants to be alone with Henri, who, he infers, has already achieved his ends, but complies. With Pauline at the beach, he seems to take up Marion's earlier suggestion to court the younger cousin. He caresses Pauline, and his odd behavior, when a friend of Sylvain appears and Pauline asks him about her friend, renders Pauline suspicious. She circles around him, and after some hesitation he tells now on Sylvain, as he had told before on Henri. She does not believe him, and this gives them the excuse to go to Henri's villa, where they rightly presume Marion to be, whom they inconvenience considerably since she has to come down topless. Marion and Henri confirm Pierre's story, while reproaching him for causing Pauline's sobbing. While Henri adds new lies and even perjury, Marion observes him and pats her cousin. The humiliated Pierre leaves but meets by chance Louisette, who, after some hesitation, confesses to him the truth, for she too does not love to be manipulated. When she tries to get a date with Pierre, he is both embarrassed and flattered, and she is disappointed that he manages to find an excuse. The cousins are leaving with their car when Sylvain arrives at Henri's villa, but they depart refusing to speak with him. He is justifiably angry, but Henri condescendingly explains to him that Pierre was the one who told Pauline, that he himself does not want to make people cry (we remember Jérôme), and that there is no reason to make Marion now cry too after Pauline was sobbing. He feels sympathy and tenderness for Marion but love is over in his life, and Louisette is at least exciting. In the meanwhile, the two cousins sit in their own garden in front of flowers, discussing love in shot reverse shot. When Marion declares that she will make Henri fall very deeply in love with her, she laughs in an excited, self-deluding way— and we join in this laughter, because we have just heard what Henri thinks about her. Pauline does not laugh but she smiles. A telegram calls Marion back to Paris for one day, and on the way to the railway station she stops at Henri's villa. But the door is closed this time. The image of her, writing on her knees a note, in front of the inaccessible building is a powerful symbol of the closure of their relationship (and a sign that Henri's openness has its limits).

When Pierre comes to visit, Pauline is reading a then-popular detective story by Gérard Lecas in the garden. Pierre apologizes for his behavior and tells her what he has heard from Louisette. They then drive to look for Sylvain at various beaches, but Pauline does not have his address (like a later Rohmerian heroine). They eat in a restaurant, talking about the perennial topic of the film: love. Pauline again shows good sense but Pierre feeds on revenge phantasies, and his smiles show that while obsessed with Marion he does not exclude flirting with Pauline. There is something histrionic in his behavior, and again a plant behind his back reminds us, even in a restaurant, of nature's simplicity when compared with human duplicity. Suddenly, Henri and Sylvain come down from the upper floor of the restaurant (staircases stand for both separation and connection of two worlds), and the company moves to his villa, where Henri offers champagne and even invites Sylvain to tell Marion the truth. But Sylvain does not want to be like Pierre, and this remark as well as the ensuing question of who should bring the kids home even leads to a physical fight between Pierre and Sylvain, Henri, as usual, being the observer and Pauline being pulled by the two men. Irritated, she decides that Sylvain should drive home with Pierre and that she will accept Henri's invitation to sleep in his villa, because she is afraid of being alone in her own house. Pierre is aghast (his face changed already when Henri extended his kind offer to stay overnight) but Henri reassures everybody with a shameless face that he is not the wolf, and he lets Pauline withdraw upstairs to sleep in the room where she had already been with Sylvain some days before.

The next morning Henri is awakened by a phone call, which, however, proves as beneficial to him as the one that Gaspard receives at the end of *Conte d'été*. A certain Inés informs him in Spanish that she is close by and expects him—who then declares himself free like air—the next day on her ship, which has the pretentious name *La Revoltosa* (*The Rebellious One*)—a sarcastic innuendo at those people who believe that they are promoting world revolution by sexual promiscuity. Henri manages to prepone the appointment to the same day in order to avoid seeing Marion again, and in a black bathrobe, which stresses his infernal traits, he walks over to Pauline's room. Pauline is deeply asleep, and one has to recognize that the image of her, lying, wearing only minimal underwear and bare-breasted, as she had been when making out with Sylvain on the same bed, now, however, partially under a sheet, is one of the most erotic ones in Rohmer's œuvre. Henri begins to kiss her feet and moves upward, till she awakens and kicks him off. It is important to look at the objects in Pauline's sleeping-room: she lies under a reproduction of Henri Matisse's *La Blouse Roumaine*, whose white shirt reminds us of the white nightgown in which Pauline stepped into the garden on her first morning and which is a symbol of purity. A small child's bed, in which Marie must have slept when she was younger, contributes to the atmosphere of innocence. On another wall, a red life ring is hanging, and while it is connected to Henri's ideal of restless mobility, it evokes at the same time the hope that Pauline may be saved from drowning. But it is absolutely crucial to recognize the iconological reference hidden in the body of the sleeping Pauline. It is so paradoxical that it does not really come as a surprise that it has not yet been noticed,[8] but once one perceives it, it becomes so obvious that one asks oneself how one could have overlooked it. It may help to begin with Henri's kiss. This peculiar kiss does not simply point to another form of partialism; it reminds a Catholic of the kiss of the foot of the Pope. But who is the Pope? The Vicar of Christ. And now finally the curtain falls: Pauline's almost naked body, partly covered by a sheet, but clothed only with underwear, is an evocation of the dead Christ with only a loincloth on his shroud. A model for Rohmer may have been the painting *Le Christ mort couché sur son linceul* (*The Dead Christ Lying on His Shroud*) in the Louvre by Philippe de Champaigne, who is mentioned in *Conte de printemps* and whose links to Jansenism must have enticed Rohmer. But even if the formal similarity is granted, what has Pauline to do with Christ? We already saw that the beginning of the story is about the fall; and for a Catholic like Rohmer, the fall is not the last word but redemption has to follow. Pauline's sudden awakening and sitting up with her eyes so stunned as if they had looked at something belonging to another world is an equivalent of the resurrection, even if at the same time she covers her breasts with her sheet; and her disabling kick against a figure in whom we already recognized an analogue of the devil corresponds to Christ's triumph over death. Death, however, is connected with sin;[9] and Pauline overcomes sin not simply by not complying with the role model of the grown-ups, but by the care which she shows immediately afterwards even for Henri, whom she believes hurt and who first tries to excuse his behavior claiming that he wanted to wake her up in a sweet manner before he acknowledges that she is a woman and he a man. No less touching is Pauline's care for Marion, when during breakfast Henri tells her that he is about to depart and without looking at her hands over his letter of good-bye for Marion. In order to justify himself, he even quotes Huxley's *Brave New World*, generously forgiving Pauline for not knowing it: Marion's body is so perfect that it would bore him if every woman became like her, and while physically committed to her, in his mind he was always desiring Louisette more, whom, furthermore, he had met first. His wish to avoid seeing Marion is simply based on the fact that he does not love goodbyes—a sentence later repeated by Marion, who thus manifests in a comic way that the couple indeed shared something. But we already know from Sabine and Edmond that this is not sufficient to make a good couple. After handing over the letter, Pauline will ask Marion to leave and return to Paris. Listening with lowered eyes and a shy smile to Marion's generous offer that each of the two women should believe that Louisette was with the other woman's lover, Pauline agrees with such tact and grace that we understand why this girl can represent Christ. She may have lost her naïvety in this story of coming of age, but her basic goodness redeems her, and potentially us viewers, if we are able to understand this story in all its depth.

Even in film, transpositions of Christian iconography into secular contexts are old; Hitchcock's allusion to the Deposition from the Cross in *The Lodger*, when the innocent hero is taken down from the railing on which his handcuffs have entangled him by the mob ready to lynch him, is well known.[10] Rohmer's earlier allusions to the Bible were of this type. Certainly, Robert Bresson's *Au hasard Balthazar* rose to a new level by offering the life of a donkey as an imitation of Christ; but also here the religious allusions, particularly in the death scene, are readily recognizable. The transformation of the dead male body of Christ into a sleeping female beauty running the danger of being raped, however, is even more daring and possibly insulting for many Christians. One might mention Richard Wagner's *Tristan und Isolde* (*Tristan and Isolda*) when discussing the connection between death and erotic desire, which share the overcoming of the boundaries of individuality, but Wagner is hardly a Christian. Rohmer, however, does not simply play with the Christian imagery but remains committed to basic Christian values; all eroticism notwithstanding, what he feels for Pauline is charity and a true concern for her moral well-being. One might object that only the Catholic suppression of sexuality could bring a person to the point that he perceived a corpse where a beautiful girl lies, or, rather, that he permitted himself to work on the later image to hint at the dead Christ. The objection is intelligen, but one should answer that this is exactly the reason why Catholicism has brought forth so much great art: for great art needs both a sensuous element, wrongly rejected by the Jansenists, and its transcendence, abolished in the age of naturalism. The miraculous grace of Rohmer's films consists in the ease in which a smoothly narrated story about beach sex is at the same time a story about fall and salvation. For *Pauline* is no less a religious film than *Ma nuit chez*

Maud, even if there are no explicit theological discussions and even if we do not see any character enter a church (only Mont Saint-Michel abbey is shown from afar, where Pauline may have gained strength). Hermetic art makes it immediately obvious that we have to search for a deeper meaning (sometimes, the meaning may not even be there, but the work at least gets attention by pretending to have it), yet Rohmer's *Pauline* is not hermetic at all. No absurdity in it forces us to look at an allegorical meaning, and of the many viewers of it[11] the overwhelming majority enjoyed it for the funny story and its French eroticism.[12] But if eroticism has to do with the search for deeper strata of the beloved, then an *erotic interpretation* is one that is not fooled by the surface but looks beneath it.[13] We will need much more research before all of Rohmer's religious references are understood, hidden as they are under the realist depiction of contemporary erotic life.

7

Rohmer the Non-Moralizing Moralist

Rohmer's realism is, I said, non-naturalistic. This is true on three different levels. First, Rohmer sees the various parts of reality as interconnected and uses physical objects or events as symbols of mental states. This in itself is not original; metaphors live from such transitions between the physical and the mental. But as early as 1955, Rohmer noted that most poetical metaphors had become stale, to a large amount due to the ascent of modern technology and due to the collapse of the teleological worldview that connected the various parts of the universe into an integral order. He remains committed, however, to such a view and even argues that the ultimate harmony between nature and human work is the best, and perhaps only, access to an understanding of the divine order.[1] While Balázs rightly insists that the landscape in a film has to be an organic part of the story, he wrongly infers that filming is best done in a studio.[2] Such an inference, however, is no longer plausible if, with Rohmer, one believes in an ultimate harmony of nature and spirit. By presenting real images, the film can revitalize the metaphoric power—it is natural to interpret the walk among the ruins of Pompeii in Rossellini's *Journey to Italy* as an expression of the frailness of the marriage of the two main characters.[3] In Rohmer's own films, to give some examples, the opening and closing of the garden gate in *Pauline* stands, as we saw, for a closed episode in Marion's life, the apple Pauline was eating for her erotological awakening. Pierre's windsurfing symbolizes the difficulties of navigating erotic relations; the life ring symbolizes Pauline's salvation from rape; the mirror in Frédéric's office in *L'Amour l'après-midi* symbolizes his dreamy narcissism; and the algae moving in the sea of *La Collectionneuse* symbolize the atmosphere of being driven by the elementary force of sexual desire. Note that the gate, the girl eating her apple, the surfboard, the life ring, the mirror, and the algae are all captured in their specific qualities and beauty; they are not simply signs standing for something else. Where this happens, the quality of the film inevitably suffers.[4] The pens with which François at the beginning of *La Femme* has difficulties writing are, on the other hand, not fascinating in themselves; their symbolic meaning, pointing to François' sexual frustration, is too obvious and has been so often used (think only of Madame Chauchat's seduction of Hans Castorp in the last scene of the fifth chapter of *Der Zauberberg* (*The Magic Mountain*)) that it can only elicit a yawn.

Despite his refusal to depict mental life as such, Rohmer interprets nature as pointing toward the mind. The mind, however, is by its essence evaluating. Rohmer is thus a moralist in a double sense—he unravels the intricate nature of our soul, the self-deception at work behind our moralizing, but at the same time remains committed to the belief in an objective moral order. Because he firmly considers adultery a breach of trust and thus morally wrong, he can rejoice in Frédéric's return to Hélène or in Jeanne's rejection of Igor. The intellectual and moral tensions of his heroes and heroines would evaporate in the moment in which we embraced a naturalistic understanding of sexuality, as merely an art of increasing physical pleasure. The extraordinary erotic intensity of Rohmer's films is a result of two factors—on the one hand, the French appreciation of intelligent flirtation and the post-Freudian recognition of the omnipresence of sexual desire in human behavior; on the other hand, the defense of the moral ideal that sexual intercourse should express love and crown a commitment between two persons. The absence of an explicit moral condemnation in a film does not entail that the director does not pass a judgment—on the contrary, the judgment is the more powerful if it imposes itself on the viewer of the film without even being insinuated by a single concrete image. The fact that we do not see Jacqueline's disappointment at the end of the first film of the cycles is an excellent filmic decision because we thus have to represent it ourselves—and by perceiving its absence we grasp the rudeness of the self-righteous narrator, who does not want to see the suffering he has caused. And if someone does not notice this absence and only focuses on the reunion with Sylvie? Well, then he has not understood the point of the film, and it was not made for him. Rohmer's main characters do not always abstain from moral judgments—that would be very unrealistic indeed. But their judgments are rarely those of the director, who may rather side with the elder generation of the parents (such as Sabine's mother) or the teenagers (such as Pauline) than with the young adults in love.

Even more important than explicit assertions is the poetic justice that most of Rohmer's sixteen erotic films display.[5] (This does not hold for his historical films; on the contrary, in *Triple Agent* Rohmer transformed the historical Nikolai Skoblin's bolshevist wife Nadezhda Plevitskaya, who most probably was responsible for making him change sides and work for the NKVD, into the Greek Arsinoe, an innocent victim of her husband's, Fiodor Voronin's, duplicity or triplicity, which she only in the course of the film comes to suspect. The harsh sentencing and early death of Arsinoe is thus a manifest injustice.) The people whom Rohmer morally dislikes usually fail; the ones whom he admires have a better chance to be blessed by luck in their erotic quest. Maud and Chloe remain alone, Sabine and Marion do not get what they want, and Louise falls victim to the principle she herself was advancing. Jean-Louis and Françoise and perhaps Claire and Gilles, Rémi and Marianne, Delphine and the cabinet-maker whom she meets under the auspices of the green ray, Fabien and Blanche, Magali and Gérald, Félicie and Charles fare better. Whether their union will work out, Rohmer artfully leaves open, for he knows full well that the success of a marriage is the work of a lifetime and that a mere ending with a wedding, like in traditional comedy, does not solve the hard question: will this marriage endure? But at least we have reason for rational hope. Poetic justice does not exclude that rather positive characters remain alone—I mention only Pierre, who is far from faultless, and Loïc, one of Rohmer's most endearing characters. There is also the opposite phenomenon that people cordially disliked by Rohmer seem to triumph. Jérôme leaves reveling about his good deed, but he is objectively wrong about the situation, and we have reason to doubt that his marriage to Lucinde will be a happy one. Henri starts for the next adventure, but although we can predict for him still a lot of good sex (for some women like him), the shallowness of the character will remain an indelible mark.

Denying that Rohmer's characters have different moral levels is absurd, but four factors mitigate his moral stance. First, like the Italian Neorealists Rohmer tries to understand the world as it is before he passes judgment. There is some nostalgia for the old Catholic sexual morality, but Rohmer knows that in Western Europe it has almost evaporated, even in Catholic circles. Félicie's worry that Loïc's conservative Catholic parents would dislike him marrying a single mother are dismissed with the remark: "You know, in our times ..." But Rohmer does not simply submit to the change of times. There is no doubt that he sides with his Félicie, whose moral and even religious intensity is far superior to that of all other characters in the film, and certainly to that of the moralizer of the first tale. Second, in his three cycles Rohmer does not really represent evil persons. Several of his characters are superficial, lascivious, faithless, dishonest, jealous, and envious, but none enjoys gratuitous cruelty. There is no Iago or Valmont in Rohmer's universe, and therefore he does not reverse the death of tragedy so well diagnosed by George Steiner. True enough, the sadness that we feel for Louise is even greater when she immediately calls the next erotic pretender, but this does not change the fact that she will not suffer much: she lacks the depth for that. Unlike an earlier version of the novella that became *Le genou*, the sixteen films do not present anything palpably devastating; there is no suicide of a rejected lover, no abortion (luckily, people have learnt to use contraceptives efficiently), not even a venereal disease. Sex is often loveless, but never violent—even Henri stops after Pauline's formidable kick. Despite the latter's diabolic traits, it would be an insult to Valmont's intelligence, strength of will, and physical prowess to compare him with the banal beach seducer: after the collapse of Catholicism, Marion's conquest is considerably less demanding than that of the Présidente de Tourvel, and with regard to Pauline, Henri fails, while the childish Cécile de Volanges, alas, lacks both Pauline's knowledge about sex and the elasticity of her legs to ward off rape. By ignoring crimes and the side-effects of sexuality, Rohmer can focus on the intrinsic value, positive and negative, of erotic relations. In doing so, he represents loneliness and self-deceit; and he shows us that navigating the ocean of sexuality easily leads to emotional shipwreck. But he does not present any catastrophe; even natural death is avoided.[6] Third, Rohmer does not deny that every person is prone to sin.[7] On the contrary, the Catholic beauty ogled in Notre-Dame du Port has contributed to the destruction of a marriage; the honorable wife and mother concerned for her friend's welfare enjoys her self-imposed intermediary work much more than one would like to grant. Still, one must be blind not to see the moral difference between the repentant Françoise, who even during her adulterous affair was in love, and someone like Sabine, who is essentially incapable of love. Fourth, Rohmer does not tire of insisting that finding the right partner is ultimately a stroke of luck—or a gift of grace.[8] No doubt there are necessary conditions for a stable partnership, but even together they are not sufficient. Successful erotic love must be *reciprocal* and *based on a stable friendship*; and the latter can only exist when people are both at ease with each other, know each other, and respect the values incarnated in the other. Friendship and lasting love are easier if people are similar to each other, because only so will they share interests in the long run; but at the same time erotic attraction is often directed toward diversity. Rohmer insists that *the element of erotic attraction is indeed indispensable for love*. Félicie likes Loïc, but she does not reciprocate his erotic love, and he has to learn that under such conditions a marriage is impossible. While there must be an emotional basis for love, an *act of will* is needed in order to generate a commitment. Such an act does not fall from heaven but has to be mediated with the life plans one has; and although Gaspard and Margot harmonize very well, they are in different developmental stages and thus not fit for each other—Margot wants to have children, Gaspard is not yet ready. The act of commitment has to be reciprocal too; but that is not sufficient, since *trust in the lasting nature of the other's will* is also needed: one has to believe in one's own and the other person's act of will. How this trust can originate after the collapse of the sacramental nature of marriage and the pervasiveness of divorce is the crucial question, and it speaks for Rohmer's honesty that he does not pretend to have an answer. As long as this is the case, marriage will remain what Ernest Renan famously called the nation: a daily plebiscite; and precariousness and fragility will only be overcome if there is trust in something greater than humans. For lasting love of a person is only possible if there is some form of love of the ultimate ground of being.

Beyond the mysterious connections between the physical and the mental and the moral coordinates for human choices that his films imply, there is a third dimension in which Rohmer's realism most radically transcends naturalism. He interprets the world as a whole as the expression of a moral principle. With the tradition of Platonism, he recognizes in the implementation of Forms one of the basic features of reality, which accounts for its beauty. But the ultimate Form for him is goodness, and using the language of Kant, he even suggests that the goodness is the only thing-in-itself. The superb final pages of his aesthetics of music[9] apply, *mutatis mutandis*, to his own films. There, Rohmer speaks about the goodness of the music of Bach, Haydn, Mozart, and Beethoven. While Mozart's goodness is deeply eroticized (it is almost inevitable to add: like that of Rohmer himself), Haydn stands for small goodness, namely bonhomie, and Bach and Beethoven for great goodness. But while Bach and Haydn are truly naïve, the naïvety of Beethoven is willed, the result of a conquest and expression of a virtue conscious of its right. This conscience, however, Rohmer hastens to add, has nothing to do with good conscience, either of the author or of the audience. For goodness is not in us but in the world or better, beyond all appearances, in its ultimate ground. Art expresses this goodness and invites us to grasp and follow it. By its example it opens up a field of freedom. We see here, I think, the lasting source of Rohmer's artistic appeal. While naturalism deprives the world of moral meaning, there is, on the other hand, a self-righteous moralism that indicts human follies and terminates in a deep contempt for the world as it is. Rohmer's specific religiosity permits him to believe in the ultimate reality of goodness and at the same time view humanity without illusions but still with compassion. Rohmer is what so few of his confreres and generally of the intellectuals of the twentieth century have been, a modernist who explores relentlessly the changes of twentieth-century humans in their most intimate behavior and a *homo religiosus* at the same time. It is this mixture of modern psychology and classical trust in being—a mixture that has its origin in the great seventeeth-century French moralists—that warrants Rohmer's status as a classic. As early as 1955 Rohmer defended the Leibnizian theory that we live in the best possible world and even claimed that the new art of film was an argument for it.[10] But it is worth remarking that, due to this philosophical conception, certain traits of Catholicism, like traditional Christology, are absent not only from Rohmer's films but even from his theoretical writings (which does not prevent but in fact enables him to integrate the image of the dead Christ into *Pauline*). In any case, it is his complex philosophical religiosity that allowed him to be a moralist without becoming a moralizer.

8

Conclusion

Rohmer's limits are quite obvious. We can list the following. First, just because of his realism, he is not the creator of new techniques of film. Whoever is attracted by formal innovations, whoever prefers films that depict nomologically impossible worlds will not be satisfied with his filmic universes. Still, I dare to predict that as abstract painting is not the future of that art, which must return again and again to concrete objects, so a non-naturalistic realism à la Rohmer, while by no means the only permissible style, will remain in the long run, if not the gold standard, one of the most lasting currencies in film aesthetics. For the world is simply too beautiful to be replaced or distorted by arbitrary constructions. And the fact that Rohmer was able to make some filmic masterpieces with a very small budget is deeply encouraging. Like architecture, film is an expensive art, and thus the autonomy of the artist is inevitably limited by the expectations of the producer and the owner of the building respectively. The revolt of the *Nouvelle Vague* against capitalist stifling of true creativity was morally and aesthetically necessary; and it is noteworthy that the most conservative of its auteurs remained very parsimonious in his filmmaking.

Second, thematically Rohmer is far less rich than other film directors. While his nine feature films only mentioned but not dealt with in this book add some new dimensions, even in them is eroticism important, and in some even the focus; and it is fair to say that that other great social relation, power, which Shakespeare has explored with no less precision than love, is beyond Rohmer's scope. Third, the erotic cycles avoid tragedy; and even the psychiatric aspects of eroticism, which so fascinated Hitchcock, do not appear on Rohmer's screen. One could mention partialism, but one will agree that it is a minor disturbance, compared with Norman Bates's or even Marnie's problems. Fourth, the completely selfless version of love is not Rohmer's topic—there is no equivalent in his films to Edit's self-sacrifice for David Holm in Victor Sjöström's *Körkarlen* (*The Phantom Carriage*) or Jeanne's unconditional waiting for Michel in Robert Bresson's *Pickpocket*. For Félicie waits only for a missing person, not for a prison inmate who has shown her often enough that he does not reciprocate her love.

Even the depiction of erotic love, fifth, does not extend beyond the boundaries of French Catholic propriety; and that is one of the reasons why Rohmer's films are less exhilarating than Woody Allen's. As a good Catholic, Rohmer is not at all socially exclusive—every person has a right to love, from the hair cutter to the philosophy teacher, from the math student to the winemaker. While the overwhelming majority of his characters are young or middle-aged, *Conte d'automne* celebrates the quest for love of people in the fall of their life. But all lovers are French—even Magali and Gérald, for being born in North Africa does not affect their Frenchness. Igor may be of Russian descent but one does not hear it when he speaks French. Aurora is a Romanian but only a friend, not a lover, of Jérôme; and her husband will be a Romanian too. French is spoken almost exclusively in the erotic cycles, if we abstract from Henri's awful Spanish at the end of *Pauline*, the grotesque pidgin English and fragments in other languages in the final part of *Le rayon vert*, and the beautiful Provençal song sung during the final moments of *Conte d'automne*. But the first two are made fun of, and Provençal is still a language of France. It is fair to say that the challenge of an intercultural erotic encounter in our time did not attract Rohmer. I say "in our time," for in *L'Anglaise et le Duc* the heroine is British (in fact Scottish, not English), and the French duke was for some time her lover.[1] The aristocratic world, true enough, was far more international than that of nationalist democracies but have we not achieved in the last quarter of the twentieth century an internationalism among the relationships of commoners that can vie with that of aristocratic circles of yore? If eroticism is enhanced by the discovery of difference, then intercultural relations may be particularly erotic. One should be cautious with criticism of Rohmer, however. An artist can only represent what he understands, and lack of interest does not entail rejection. Still, the young Rohmer's eurocentrism was quite strong,[2] the enormous achievements of Japanese film notwithstanding, and his antipathy against exotism remained pronounced all his life. The scene in *L'Ami*, however, when Blanche and Fabien take refuge from the loud beach pullulating with Northern Africans to a quieter place, is not racist. Rohmer soberly recognizes that the immigrants are the heirs of the French worker class of earlier times, and a couple in love has the right to be alone.

No less taboo is the topic of homosexual erotic love,[3] probably due to the author's Catholicism, although his own brother defended homosexuality. Only in his last film, the attraction between Astrée and Céladon, who disguises himself as a woman, on the surface reminds one of a lesbian attraction, before the true heterosexual nature of the love becomes evident. Rohmer's lack of interest in homoerotic love must be based rather on some idea of the complementarity of the two sexes than on the infertility of homosexual love, since in his own unfolding of heterosexual love reproduction is rare.

By the characters he dislikes, children are experienced mainly as burden, but even his favorite characters seldom make the transition from the couple to the family. The most important exceptions are Jean-Louis and Françoise at the end of *Ma nuit* as well as Félicie, whose bond with Charles is incarnated in Élise.[4] The exclusiveness of the dual relation even pushes the respective families of origin into the background—when they are presented, as in *Le Beau mariage*, they become quickly counterproductive. But there are no possessive parents, such as in the tradition beginning with the Hellenist New Comedy, to disturb the young generation's bliss—their problems are all self-made.

What about Rohmer's analysis of gender relations? Beginning with Joan Mellen's book, the sixth chapter of which is dedicated to the four feature films of the *Contes moraux*, Rohmer has been often attacked by feminist film theorists. The problem of such attacks is that feminism is not at all a unitary position and that often enough feminists, who start by rightly pointing out unjust asymmetries between men and women, combine with this critique other moral ideas, concerning which one may agree or disagree but that have very little to do with the issue at stake, namely an unfair treatment of women. Mellen, for example, identifies with Maud and shares her deep hatred for Françoise. "Jean-Louis at the end is doomed to a placid, predictable life with Francoise [sic!], broken only by the lies these two repressed people find necessary for the protection of their self-delusion."[5] It is not clear to me who is supposed to be able to predict their life—the couple, the director, or the film critic? If the couple settle for each other because they predict that they will have together a long and happy marriage, without divorce or emotional alienation, what is wrong? If they are so in love that they do not even think about their future, but the director or the critic can predict a happy future, I do not see any difficulty either. Is Mellen disappointed because Maud, whom she admires, does not get the man she desires? Such is life. Vidal does not conquer Maud either, and Maud would have hardly approved if Jean-Louis had slept with her only to marry afterwards Françoise, whom he happens to love more. The repression of a sexual urge, when people know that it does not correspond to love or commitment, may be a wise thing, and certainly in the past women have often, and rightly, complained when men did not check that urge. Concerning the lies and self-delusion, either we speak about different films, or tact is a form of lie. Jean-Louis is honest about his earlier affairs to both Maud and Françoise, and not at their first date, but quite early on, Françoise confesses her own relation to Jean-Louis, even if without naming the person whom she has no reason to believe Jean-Louis could be connected with. That he does not return to the topic but respects her wish to keep silent about it is a sign of his love, as is his final insinuation (he does not explicitly lie) that he had an affair with Maud. One may believe that the continuous scratching of the psychic wounds of one's partner makes humans happier, stronger, perhaps morally better, but it is at least not obvious that it always does. If Jean-Louis had chosen to show Françoise that he now had found out whose lover she had been, other critics would probably have discovered in it a male desire of domination and humiliation, and probably with better reasons. Mellen values risky behavior, satisfaction of sexual urges, and lack of discretion, and that is her right. But since autonomy probably belongs to her values, too, she should recognize that there are people, including women, who make different choices. It is probably a good idea that people rather marry persons with similar values, and thus a feminist should rejoice that Françoise has found the right husband.

No doubt, the six *Contes moraux* are written from the perspective of a male narrator. This introduces an asymmetry, but it is an asymmetry inevitably connected with the choice of an individual narrator, who in the overwhelming majority of cases has to be either male or female. That in all cases the narrator is male follows from the central aesthetic idea of varying a basic structure; an alternation of the gender of the narrator was not compatible with it. And that Rohmer chose the male instead of the female perspective is, given his own gender, quite natural. Artists should write about what they know best; and men usually are more familiar with male than with female desire. Concerning the characters of these and the other films, however, Rohmer seems to me as generous as possible toward the female sex. There is not the least bias toward the narrator, who on the contrary is regularly deconstructed (with the exception of Jean-Louis). It is obvious that in the first story the director sides with Jacqueline, not the narrator; and if this is interpreted as a sign of Rohmer's condescendence toward female weakness, already the second tale displays with Suzanne a woman more mature than the narrator. Maud is intellectually superior to Vidal, Adrien more intolerable than Haydée, Jérôme a zero compared with the triad of Aurora, Laura, and Claire, each fascinating in her own right. Only a haphazard event saves Frédéric from Chloe, who manipulates him at will; and the noblest character of the last moral tale is doubtless Hélène. Poor François is at the mercy of Anne; Sabine is truly disagreeable, but Edmond hardly less; the hero of the third comedy is a girl; and Rémi's revenge is by a man who has endured enough humiliations by his woman. No character in the cycles receives so much attention as Delphine, a Félicie *avant la lettre*, who does not want to lower her standards for love, even if she is not committed to any concrete person. Blanche and Fabien are soul mates, but Blanche is more conscientious when dealing with Léa. Jeanne may have an innate female sense of orderliness but she is the most intellectual person in the film, as a philosopher superior to the bookish Loïc. Gaspard may be the winner in the summer game in Dinard, but Margot is one of the most enchanting creations of Rohmer. Isabelle and Rosine are far more active than the men,[6] and Félicie is the character in Rohmer's films with the strongest determination.[7] If we look at the two historical tragedies dealing with the French and the aftermath of the Soviet revolution, in both cases it is the woman who proves to have the superior moral instinct, while the men shipwreck because of their opportunism. If there is a lack of balance in Rohmer's work, then it is only because he finds women in most cases more resourceful, more passionate, and more subtle than men. In none of his films is there something like the taming of the shrew by a dominant man, characteristic of various Hitchcock movies, from *Notorious* to *Marnie*.

The main reason why Rohmer's films will stay with us is that this conservative Catholic has offered the most precise panorama of modern erotic life in all its physical and mental iridescence. While his topic is much narrower than that of other great directors, its importance in human life can hardly be overrated; and the intensity with which he illuminates it on both the descriptive and normative levels is unmatched by any other director. No doubt, Rohmer draws from a French culture of eroticism that started as early as the Middle Ages and for centuries now has permeated both French everyday life and its high culture; and no less is he indebted to authors such as La Rochefoucauld and Pascal in his acute description of human psychology. This explains why his work has been successful particularly in France. But since erotic life does not seem to be limited to French people, Rohmer's œuvre has the same claim to universal attention as has, for example, Stendhal's *De l'amour* (*On love*): he is a classic of late modernity. As long as the fragile nature of modern relationships between man and woman is not overcome (and nothing short of a religious revolution is needed to achieve that), Rohmer's work will remain a compass in the labyrinth of eroticism and continue to entice through its extraordinary sense for beauty in nature and human interactions, its fine human tact, its ironical but never spiteful persiflage of contemporary vices, and its intelligent and discreet religiosity.

Notes

Preface

1. See the intelligent analysis of the recent debate in Sinnerbrink (2011), 117–35. The discussion, however, suffered from the lack of familiarity with the great aesthetical theories of the past and its limitation to film: most of the pro and con arguments hold also for the relation between philosophy and literature. In general, a problem of much of film aesthetics in the twentieth century consists in the fact that, fascinated by the specific originality of film, it neglects its roots in a general theory of the beautiful and the arts.

2. The reasons for the use of the pseudonym were various, but an important one was that Schérer did not want his mother to find out about her son being a film director (she thought he had remained a teacher). She died in 1970 without realizing that her son had become an international celebrity. See the authoritative Rohmer biography by de Baecque and Herpe (2014: 237). In general, Rohmer was shy and very reserved about himself.

3. The essay is dedicated to Chaplin's last film, *A Countess from Hong Kong*, in which he himself plays only a cameo role (Bazin and Rohmer 1972: 106–22; Bazin et al. 1985: 73–89).

4. On Godard, see Rohmer's affectionate but ironic remarks (2010), 140f., 171.

5. It was reprinted in 2007 with the title *La maison d'Elisabeth* and has been translated into German and Spanish but not yet into English. The text anticipated features of the nouveau roman but Rohmer later rejected it, in part because he understood that he could not make a good film out of it. Paradoxically, he came to the conclusion that he needed to integrate conversations on non-frivolous matters to be truly realistic (2013: 35).

6. Already in 1948, his collaboration with *Les Temps Modernes*, founded

by Jean-Paul Sartre and Simone de Beauvoir, ended when he wrote in a review that, because of the dialectical nature of history, conservative values will become more modern than progressive ones: Rohmer (1984), 11f./ (1989), 4. In 1955, he calls himself first "classic by instinct" (2010: 33) and asks then with remarkable self-assurance "Am I classic, am I modern?" (80). His answer is that he wants to unite the virtues of both ages.

7   What Rohmer and Chabrol write about Hitchcock (1979: 25; 2011: 39) holds also of Rohmer: "But he refuses and will continue to refuse to sermonize, to proselytize—so much so that audiences were quickly to forget the essentially Catholic nature of his work." See also 128/129.

8   A daughter born out of wedlock from an affair with a Danish woman demonstrates, however, that Rohmer did know sexual temptations himself.

9   Rohmer's interest in Kleist, whose *Das Käthchen von Heilbronn* he translated and performed for the stage in 1980 in Nanterre, is rooted in Kleist's discovery of the problem of how we can trust, particularly but not exclusively, in erotic relations. For Kleist, sentiment has to replace the failure of reason.

10 Tester (2008) differentiates what I call "isolated films" into two groups, period films and occasional films. The latter play in the present, too, but do not form part of a cycle.

1: The Nature of Contemporary Eroticism: Between Art of Seduction and Nostalgia for the Unconditional

1   See Hösle (2005) for a philosophical interpretation of the Darwinian theory of sexual selection.

2   The idea that love can occur only outside of marriage, since legal rights are incompatible with true love, is stated as early as May 1, 1174 in the famous letter by Marie of France, Countess of Champagne, quoted at the end of the seventh dialogue in the sixth chapter of the first book of Andreas Capellanus's *De amore*.

3   Rohmer, at least, claimed in 1955 that Renoir was the greatest French film director (2010: 29).

4   Ch. 6 (1972: 64ff.).

5   Ch. 1 (1994: I 97ff.).

6   (1998a), 76ff.

2: *Six contes moraux*

1 See the theoretically important "Avant-Propos" in Rohmer (1974), 9–14/ (1980), v–x.

2 The unreliability of a narrator can consist of outright falsehoods narrated, important facts withheld (for a selection is inevitable in every narration), and wrong moral evaluations. The unreliability may originate in deliberate mendacity, self-deception, and intellectual and/or moral limitations. In Rohmer, self-deception in evaluating one's own actions is the most frequent source. The burden of proof for the unreliability of a narrator is always with the critic who claims it, and since the critic has no independent access to the world depicted by the narrator, only internal inconsistencies or contradictions with basic moral principles can justify the verdict "unreliable." Postmodern literary criticism has wrongly declared the unreliable narrator ubiquitous, thus gambling away important differences between various texts and films.

3 See Bonitzer (1991), 102.

4 The model may be the one hundred and twenty-fifth letter in Laclos (1964: 331ff.). An author as early as Ovid likes to compare the courting with military service (*Amores* I 9, 1ff.; II 10, 29ff.), while at the same time suggesting love as a bloodless alternative to war (II 12, 5ff.; III 2, 49f.).

5 The third in the order of the tales was produced after the fourth, because Jean-Louis Trintignant, who played the hero, was not available earlier. Maud is played by Françoise Fabian, Vidal by Antoine Vitez, who at the time was a convinced communist himself. For the role of Françoise, Rohmer chose the yet unknown Marie-Christine Barrault, who, not unlike Valmont's victims, had recently come out of a convent school (see de Baecque and Herpe 2014: 210). She had only played theater a little under her famous uncle's supervision and had appeared in one TV film. But Rohmer's instinct for quality actors did not lead him astray.

6 (1955), 67ff.

7 This does not exclude the use of the wager also in *Conte d'hiver* (and in Rohmer's only drama *Le Trio en mi bémol* (1988: 28f.). On Rohmer's complex relation to the wager, see Robic (2013), 23ff., who points to important formal similarities between *Ma nuit* and *Conte d'hiver*: in both films, an event separated by five years from the rest is narrated, in the first at the end, in the second at the beginning of the film; in both, the main action takes place during Christmastime. The wager shows its power only when extended over time.

8   I am aware of the fact that this is only said in the text (1974: 71; 1980: 59), not in the film. But as Rohmer writes (1974: 13; 1980: IX), what has been dropped from the text has been eliminated only because the image already expressed it. And indeed Trintignant plays overwhelmingly well both Jean-Louis's natural self-assurance and the Catholic inhibition when it comes to sexuality. While it is true that Jean-Louis goes through a process of moral maturation, it is in my eyes wrong to see his own narrative as similarly unreliable as that of the other narrators of the *Moral Tales*, as Crisp suggests (1988: 52ff.). The actor is even more impressive than the hero of the written story, for example, when answering without wavering the question about the number of his premarital relations. Crisp, whose early book grasps much of Rohmer's subtlety, has little sympathy for his Catholicism; and by making Rohmer side with Pascal, he transforms him into a Jansenist, which this lover of physical as well as moral beauty never wanted to be, even if he recognizes Pascal's psychological perspicacity. Compare Rohmer and Chabrol's assessment of Hitchcock as "an unconscious Jansenist" (1979: 78; 2011: 83), Rohmer's criticism of the puritan mistrust against the flesh in Hitchcock, Dreyer, and Fellini in the Murnau book (2000: 99), and his statement, reminiscent of Friedrich Schiller's and Max Scheler's criticism of Kant, that taste is an instinctive love for beauty, while Protestantism wrongly teaches that we have to make an effort in order to aim at the higher sphere and are naturally drawn only to the baser strata of reality (2010: 32).

9   That faithfulness based no longer on love but on self-esteem is not the worthiest situation in a marriage is true; but it is still better than floating with one's emotions. Maud and Jean-Louis agree that in such cases amour propre is at stake, but while Jean-Louis wants at least to maintain self-respect, Maud despises this wish. She must have read Jean-Paul Sartre (1943: 434f.).

10 The end, I think, makes visible where Rohmer stands, even without any information about the author. But many contemporary critics have read the ending differently: Beverly Walker at the beginning thought that Rohmer was portraying the emancipated Maud as a role model (Rohmer (2013), 28ff.), and Frank R. Cunningham, who called the final sequence "one of film's great moments" (Showalter 1993: 178), projects his own Nietzscheanism into it, which he manages to find even in Pascal: "The final shot of her [sc. Maud] is as she walks slowly and confidently up, up the slope toward the road, secure in her Nietzschean will-to-assertion … Their [sc. Jean-Louis and Françoise's] institutional Christianity is sterile when compared to Maud's ceaseless creation of value, her spontaneous and perennial openness to risk and social and intellectual involvement. … Maud envisions other human beings as ends-in-themselves, whereas the narrator tends to see them as means, such in his utilitarian view of

Pascal and Christianity." While it is a sign of Rohmer's respectful realism that both sides (or all three, if we include Vidal) are presented with sympathy and even admiration for their respective values, I am not so sure that the humanities flourish when interpreters read their own beliefs into text or films that palpably say the opposite. There may be a ceaseless creation of meaning involved, but why not assert oneself directly without instrumentalizing the creations of other people?

11 See Bonitzer (1991), 49.

12 See Chapter 2 of the first part of *L'être et le néant* (1943: 85ff.).

13 Cf. Hösle (2012), 163ff.

14 Rousseau (1964), 152f. The reference is well analyzed by Crisp (1988), 63. On the analogies with *Julie*, see Charney (1973).

15 The double translation, here and elsewhere, refers to the British and American titles, which are not always identical.

16 It is his *Le voyage autour du monde* (*A Voyage Around the World*) that, with his depiction of promiscuity in Tahiti, inspired French libertinism, which begins with Denis Diderot's famous dialogue *Supplément au voyage de Bougainville* (*Addendum to the Journey of Bougainville*).

17 The fear of aging is symptomatic of the immature lover. While in *Stages* Kierkegaard's John the Seducer teaches that the idea of woman is not exhausted by any individual woman, so that he wants to seduce as many as possible, Judge Vilhelm declares that true beauty develops only over the course of time in the eyes of the husband (1991, Vol. 7: 73 and 120).

18 Serceau (2000: 78) rightly remarks that Frédéric ultimately has the same attitude of vacation toward reality as Adrien.

3: *Comédies et proverbes*

1 Rohmer (1999), I 8.

2 See Ch. XXIII in Stendhal's *De l'amour* (1965: 76ff.).

3 Ch. 14 in Fontane (1969), 172.

4 Rohmer will show more sympathy for the female anthropologist Margot in *Conte d'été*, but probably only because she studies Brittany, not countries far away. In *Quatre Aventures de Reinette et Mirabelle* (*Four Adventures of Reinette and Mirabelle*) the Parisian Mirabelle is an anthropologist, too, and the farmer's daughter Reinette, whom she meets after a bicycle

problem on a road, shows her that there are different forms of human life quite close to Paris.

5   Pauline does not know that she is reiterating a basic tenet of medieval philosophy of love. In his *Art amativa (Art of love)*, Ramon Llull insists on knowledge and love having to go hand in hand (1933: 4, 364).

6   The fact that it is the woman who conceives a possibility and the man who then implements it is, despite Louise's defeat, a subtle inversion of traditional role models, as Guérin (2007: 86) rightly notes.

7   On the importance of the telephone in Rohmer, see Serceau (2000), 83ff. It is the instrument appropriate to characters always on the move.

8   (1999), II 55.

9   The term "intertextuality" is not unproblematic in the case of references from a film to a film, and even to a text, since films are more than texts. Since references to artworks of the same type happen also in the visual arts and in music, it would be useful to coin terms that cover both the general phenomenon (perhaps "intermediality" is best) and its concrete manifestations in the various arts. As a synthetic art, film can refer both to other films as well as to paintings, music, and literature.

10 As early as 1955, Rohmer called Goethe's novel "perhaps the most perfect monument of world literature" (2010: 73).

11 It becomes more touching than comic when both parties want to do each other a particular favor and by doing so render not the gift, but the material value of the gift, obsolete, as in O. Henry's *The Gift of the Magi*. Some of the magic of this story is echoed in Rohmer's drama *Trio*.

4: *Contes de quatre saisons*

1   The back cover of Rohmer (1998b) contains an important reflection on the unity of the cycle by Rohmer, which inspires the beginning of what follows.

2   I do not count the unachieved 1952 feature film *Les Petites filles modèles*.

3   It is a form of the drama of reconciliation, so well defended by Roche (1997).

4   On the various parallels between Shakespeare's romance and Rohmer's film, see Cavell (2005), 289. Particularly acute is the observation that Félicie's hairdressing corresponds to sheep shearing in Shakespeare.

5: The Idea of a Realist Cinema

1. See the interview with Rohmer: (2007), 213f.

2. Compare Rohmer (1974), 14.

3. Rohmer (1984), 37–40 and (1989), 29–33.

4. Rohmer is not fair when he bases the superiority of film over theater on the fact that only the former lasts (2010: 28f.). This has nothing to do with the aesthetic value of the two arts but with their nature. Film and painting are one-stage arts, music and drama are two-stage arts (see Goodman 1976: 113f.), and performance is necessarily temporal. Thanks to film, we can reproduce theater performances almost as well as music performances (I say "almost" because of the dimensional loss involved in the first but not in the second case). In this case, however, film is only used as a medium, no longer as an independent art with its own laws. On film and theater, Sontag' s essay (1991: 99–122) remains inspiring.

5. See the discussion reported by Arnheim in his 1932 classic (1933: 201ff.; 2002: 189ff.).

6. In his essay "The Ontology of the Photographic Image," Bazin writes: "All the arts are based on the presence of man, only photography derives an advantage from his absence" (2005: I 9–16, 13; 1990: 9–17, 13). Rohmer agrees (1998a: 102f.) and rightly insists (2010: 16) that the emancipation of the visual arts from the mimetic task became possible only because of photography (not the other way around). He calls photography a minor art because it only partly succeeds in the reproduction of reality, whose life, unlike film, it cannot capture (2010: 43). It is worth mentioning that Arnheim, who in his seminal book strongly insisted on the creativity of film, which alone could make it an art, in his 1978 preface to a new German edition recognized the combination of mechanical reproduction and artistic choice as the peculiar feature of film, explicitly acknowledging the work by Bazin and Siegfried Kracauer (2002: 11f.). But Arnheim's focus on the differences between reality and photographic/filmic image—differences due to the loss of one dimension as well as to the fact that the image has formal properties of its own, alien to the object reproduced—remains important. Neglecting it, as does Bazin, is unilateral as well.
   In his excellent overview and critique of classical film theory (1988), Noël Carroll, probably the best American film theorist alive, has rightly treated Arnheim and Bazin as the two central and opposite figures in the early philosophy of film. He includes in his work also Perkins (1972), who wants to offer a metacritical stance that overcomes the essentialist limitations of the earlier approaches, which tend to favor only a specific type of film. What is still missing in film theory, however, is an objective

idealist approach inspired by Hegel's aesthetics that transcends both realism and constructivism by appealing to an ideal sphere.

7   Compare Rohmer (2000), 42. For a defense of beauty in mathematics and nature, see the essays in the first part of Hösle (2013).

8   One of Rohmer's various films for television was dedicated in 1968 to "Louis Lumière." I reproduce some of the ideas developed there. What Jean Renoir states in this film, namely, that at the beginning of a new art you need not be an extraordinary mind in order to produce astonishing artworks, because the new possibilities elicit brilliant innovations at every step, holds also for film theory. The first books in this new field of aesthetics have hardly been surpassed in their categorical precision, their enthusiasm, and their still living connection with the great European aesthetic tradition. Newer works of film aesthetics, such as Frampton (2006), often suffer from jargon and too strong a reliance on trendy French postmodernist philosophers, who tend to base far too generic theses on well-known phenomena, such as the limits of intentionalism in hermeneutics. For an overview of recent philosophies of film, see Mullarkey (2009).

9   Therefore, documentary films remain a noble task of the art of film. In so-called docu-fictions, such as Luchino Visconti's *La Terra trema* (*The Earth Trembles*), fictional stories are integrated into material filmed as a documentary of the actual world. Completely different is the fictional documentary (or mockumentary), a fictional film that pretends to be a documentary, such as Woody Allen's *Zelig*. Its possibility follows from the capacity of fiction to imitate everything, even truth claims; the mockumentary is the filmic analogue of novels that pretend to be based on historical manuscripts. Despite the enormous difference between docu-fiction and fictional documentary, a part of Rohmer's *L'arbre, le maire et la médiathèque ou les sept hazards* seems to unite features of both: there is a fictional story about a journalist who interviews local people from our actual world about their predicament.

10 In such a case, the identification of actor and character, found even among brilliant minds such as Panofsky (1967), becomes unbearable. While it is possible to say "Buster Keaton as Jimmy Shannon (in *Seven Chances*) runs," it is absurd to say "Henry Fonda as Frank (in Sergio Leone's *Once Upon a Time in the West*) kills and dies." One could only say "Henry Fonda as Frank acts as if he were killing and dying." Even if it is true that the impersonation of a character by a film actor is more permanent than that by a theater actor, it does never constitute an identity.

11 I am heavily influenced by the last chapter, dedicated to film, in Ingarden (1962: 319–41; 1989: 317–42). Regrettably, Ingarden never worked out his sketch to a volume comparable to his splendid analysis of the literary

work of art, even if the film is a far more complex art, entailing many more problems of formal ontology. Ingarden's cinematic education did not match his literary one, and he ignores important concrete issues, such as those connected to shots and editing. Still, it is his work that remains the gold standard for questions involving the ontology of the artwork, and it is a pity that mainstream film scholars rarely read him.

12 Therefore, a demarcation between the fictional and the real world is needed. In the case of paintings it is the frame, and Bazin is only partially correct when in the essay "Painting and Cinema" he radically distinguishes between the frame of the painting and the screen (2005: I 164–9, 165f.; 1990: 187–92, 188). The main difference is, of course, that the continuous movement of the image in a film leads the audience to transcend it in their expectation. But it remains a movement, so to speak, *within* the screen—namely, within the possible world constituted by it, never transgressing its borders with the actual world.

13 Of course, beginning with J. Stuart Blackton and Émile Cohl, there have also existed animated films, where the moved images are not photographs, not to speak of more recent possibilities of computer graphics. But for the purpose of this book, I limit myself to films based on photography.

14 See Lewis (1978). Lewis, however, does not answer the question of why the possible worlds created by artists allow us to understand basic features of the actual world. This is linked to his rejection of any preferential status for the actual world (or any other).

15 This intermediate position explains why in a film the single picture, like the single tone in a melody, is not seen as isolated but interpreted in the context of the earlier and following ones. Think of the famous Kuleshov effect: the same shot of the face of Ivan Mosjoukine was "read" differently according to the object that was represented in the next shot. Suspense lives from expectations that have been created by earlier shots, while, on the other hand, laughter reacts to a surprise. Both modes can only be grasped by considering the temporal context.

16 See §41 in Edmund Husserl's *Ideen zu einer reinen Phänomenologie und phänomenologischen Philosophie* (*Ideas Pertaining to a Pure Phenomenology and to a Phenomenological Philosophy*).

17 (2010), 66. Walter Ruttmann's *Berlin: Die Sinfonie der Großstadt* (*Berlin: Symphony of a Metropolis*) remains a classic example of the music of the montage.

18 See Rohmer (2000), 6f. on the first three elements. While the aesthetic enjoyment is holistic, the thorough analyst of a film is well advised to look at the various elements separately, like the musicologist who forces himself

to listen to each single voice of a symphony abstracting from the rest. One may read only the script, or one may look at a film, the language of which one does not understand, in the original language and without using subtitles.

19 So rightly Balázs in his 1924 classic (2001a: 49ff.; 2010: 38ff.). Close-up is called "the art of emphasis" (50/39).

20 See again Balázs (2001a: 33ff.; 2010: 24ff.). Balázs is strongly influenced by the physiognomic tradition, which goes back at least to the pseudo-Aristotelean treatise *Physiognomics*, a sentence quite at the beginning of which he quotes, albeit through Goethe as intermediary (2001a: 37; 2010: 27).

21 In their reproduction, there is not even the loss of one dimension, and thus there is no equivalent of the shot, which introduces an element of subjectivity. Also for this reason, sound film is more objective than silent film.

22 One can still see a loss in the disappearance of the silent film, for as Balázs points out, silent film, by depriving humans of sound, made them similar to the rest of nature, animals, plants, and even inanimate beings, which gained life and significance (2001a: 31f.; 2010: 23). But is humanism wrong when it insists on the unique position of humans, even when they are conceived as a part of nature? And is this uniqueness not a consequence of language? All this does not deny the aesthetically obvious fact that the mature silent film had achieved a complexity that the early talkies were far from displaying. But this is true for almost all new techniques, and usually they do catch up after a while.

23 In his last work on film, Balázs speaks of an aesthetic "law of impermeability." "According to this the sound film is so full of visual images that there is little room in it for words. This is the exact opposite of the position on the Shakespearian stage. ... The sound film demands a style of weightless words" (1952: 229). I agree with two caveats. First, Balázs's "law" is not an independent principle of film aesthetics but follows for film from the basic principle that all artworks, whatever their media, have to avoid redundancies. Second, since Balázs is not familiar with Karl Bühler's seminal work on the functions of language, his statements about words are too general. While it is true that, for example, the depiction of a landscape, so important in Greek tragedy and Shakespeare's dramas, does not make sense in a film screenplay, when the landscape is already shown in the film's images, the linguistic interactions that allow us to understand both the characters' mental lives and the specific nature of their interaction are crucial for a good film. Thus, a misdescription of the landscape shown by the film might be of interest if it allows us inferences not on the landscape, for they are superfluous, but on the character of

the person uttering it. According to Arnheim, unlike literature, film uses language not as an artistic tool but as a piece of nature (1933: 212; 2002: 199). A film script will always have a lesser linguistic density than a drama, for in the latter language has to achieve more, being the only medium before the drama is performed. And even the performance on stage offers less visual data than a film.

24 Rohmer (1984), 89 and (1989), 80.

25 See Rohmer (2010), 96, 98, 168, 170. Since all translation involves a partial loss, from the crucial importance of dialogue for most sound films it follows that the scholar studying them should be able to access them in their original language. While the pictorial dimension of a film does not render this demand as absolute as in the case of literary texts, whoever violates it risks missing important nuances.

26 (2005), II 16–40, 26 and (1990), 257–85, 269.

27 See, on the sociological relevance of Rohmer, the noted sociologist of sexuality and family, Michel Bozon (2007/08).

28 (2010), 117, 141f.

29 (2010), 35, 38, 42f., 45, 63, 70, 71f., 77f.

30 (2010), 89f. There is reason to be afraid that the various Daniels of this world have by now learned the noble craft of film.

31 One will notice that several of Rohmer's implied principles recur, explicitly, in the Danish Dogme 95 manifesto and the companion "vow of chastity" (kyskhedsløfter) by Lars von Trier and Thomas Vinterberg. Needless to say, both aesthetic programs strongly differ in their ultimate aim and in their interpretation of reality.

32 A possible exception is *Perceval*. But one might say that the film gives a realistic account of the medieval worldview, including its belief in miracles. The staging alone shows that this is not a film about reality, but about a literary view on reality.

33 (2008), 90. It would be even more instructive to contrast Rohmer with Bresson, whose films are much more ascetic and thus less realistic than Rohmer's (for reality likes to luxuriate). They reduce the world to elementary formal structures in which finally, prepared by complex interior processes and never in a fortuitous way, grace can manifest itself. See Bazin's (2005: I 125–43; 1990: 107–27) and Sontag's (1978: 177–95) classic essays on Bresson.

34 (1984), 90 and (1989), 81.

35 Rohmer and Chabrol did not appreciate it (1979: 82; 2011: 86) and

suspect that it was imposed on Hitchcock by the producer (while, as early as 1930, Balázs (2001b: 94; 2010: 167) anticipated the integration of surrealist segments into a realist film). Rohmer insists early on the radical philosophical difference between the physical object and the mental image, which film has to respect (2010: 18f.). See also (2000), 81 on Murnau.

36 Alain Resnais's *Smoking/No Smoking* is different, since it represents variations of the same story that are, however, ontologically independent from each other and do not refer to a common universe, as the stories in *Rashomon* pretend to. The earlier Resnais, as in *Hiroshima mon amour* and *L'Année dernière à Marienbad* (*Last Year at Marienbad*), has an aesthetical ideal opposite to Rohmer's realism (see Biotti 2010: 59). For in these films, we remain unable to discern between reality and fiction (within the universe represented), while *Rashomon* at the end delivers access to truth—which inspires the most moral act of the film. With Kurosawa, Rohmer holds that the loss of a belief in truth must paralyze our morality; and thus, while his characters continuously lie to each other and to themselves, his images never lie (see Rohmer and Chabrol 1979: 105; 2011: 107).

37 See the fine analyses of Tortajada (1999), 199ff.

38 See (2010), 93. Rohmer quotes an argument from Émile-Auguste Chartier (usually known as Alain), who had taught philosophy at the Lycée Henri-IV in Paris, which Rohmer attended (his own philosophy teacher was a pupil of Alain). Alain exhorted his pupils to tell him the number of columns of the Panthéon, which nobody was able to do—because memory lacks the clarity of immediate perception. Balázs has a different point in mind when he complains that flashbacks destroy the unified temporal perspective and usually do not make clear, as in a novel the use of the past tense does, that they refer to another time: for images cannot be conjugated (2001a: 62; 2010: 48).

39 To be more precise, one should say the following: a later image never points to an event that is anterior to the one depicted in an earlier image. Thus, it may be either posterior or simultaneous.

40 While it is true that the images that we see during Jonathan's narration show only circumstances that truly occurred, the sequence is not only highly selective but violates the temporal order of the events and thus falsifies them. Furthermore the soundtrack that we hear has Charlotte say things that she cannot have expressed. Jonathan is not simply an unreliable narrator but the director supports him in his purpose—something Rohmer would never have done, familiar though he is with unreliable narrators.

41 *Pauline* has even some features of a ring composition, a structure known from the *Iliad*, where the first book corresponds to the last, the second to the penultimate etc. But in Rohmer's film there are numerous deviations: thus the penultimate and the antepenultimate scenes correspond to the third. Yet the two visits of Pierre at Marion's house have almost the same distance from the center.

42 In 1963 he writes that cinema is less subservient than it seems at first glance to the human body and face, even if they constitute its continuous motive (2010: 15). He was particularly proud of the addition of the dimension of nature in his film based on d'Urfé, who, as an author before Rousseau, lacked the sense for nature's beauty (2010: 101). And one has to agree that the landscape photography in his last film, occasionally reminiscent of Camille Corot, is particularly enchanting. Rohmer's love for landscape and plants, however, does not extend to animals, mostly absent from his films.

43 Theater cannot even use living animals. Beside persons, only dead objects can become physically present leitmotifs, including killed animals, like the seagull in Anton Chekhov's play.

44 One might object that in *L'Anglaise et le Duc*, Rohmer's first digital film, the architectural background is visibly unreal, since thanks to chroma keying Rohmer placed his characters into a scenery based on illustrations of Paris from the eighteenth century. But only in that way could he capture Paris as it was at the time; what he lost in one sense of realism (the illusion of reality), he gained in another (accuracy of description of an architectonic reality at a given point of time).

45 See Anderst (2014).

46 (2010), 114. Rohmer avows as a weakness, because it is a lack of charity, that he feels unease when looking at the faces of mentally handicapped people.

47 Almendros (1980), 61 and (1984), 90. Reading Almendros's six or seven chapters on the films that he shot for Rohmer increases the respect for both the man and the director. Suffice it to mention that Rohmer himself swept the floor of the set in the evening and prepared tea for the crew (64/92).

48 See de Baecque and Herpe (2014), 330.

49 (1984), 48 and (1989), 40. See also 54/45: "What we call realism is only a more scrupulous search for this beauty." Cavell narrates that in 1940 he objected to an older friend, who was critical of the integration of color into films because that made them unrealistic: "The real world is not in black and white" (90).

50 Almendros (1980), 40ff. and (1984), 59f. Almendros writes how Rohmer, while often willing to be convinced, did not tolerate a cameraman who did anything without his consent. He also avoided the use of make-up, except when the character would use it on her own.

51 See Balázs' ultimately realistic defense of color film, against his earlier stance (2001b: 107ff.; 2010: 178ff.). His reflections on why a sunset, as a dynamic event, cannot be caught by a painting but only by a film are particularly enlightening,

52 Rohmer and Chabrol (1979: 94; 2011: 97) praise *Rope* for a similar achievement: "Perhaps for the first time in cinematic history, a director tried to relate color to emotional states without departing from the strictest realism" (94). His lingering as a painter did not slow down the narrative.

53 Schilling (2007: 110) states: "Rohmer has stood at the forefront of the direct sound movement in France." Still, his early films were postsynchronized.

54 See Apuleius, *Florida*, 14 and Lactantius, *Divine Institutes*, III 15.

55 Also here one cannot help remembering Balazs' prophetic book: only film will teach us to listen to silence, which the merely visual arts cannot render because silence is not a state but an event, to be contrasted with anterior and successive sounds (2001b: 121; 2010: 190f.).

56 *Kritik der Urteilskraft* (*Critique of Judgment*) §53.

57 (1998a), 81.

58 (1998a), 109.

59 Something analogous holds even of the non-realist Murnau (Rohmer 2000: 87).

60 Rohmer even states that some great films were possible only because of their small budget (2010: 90).

61 De Baecque and Herpe (2014), 218.

62 De Baecque and Herpe (2014), 329.

63 See (2010), 123f.

64 Ronald Lee Ermey, who so masterfully played Gunnery Sergeant Hartman in Stanley Kubrick's *Full Metal Jacket*, had little acting experience and was originally hired as a technical advisor. But as a former drill instructor he was what Kubrick was looking for.

65 See Rohmer (2010), 124, 172. The actors themselves, however, experienced

Rohmer as having very clear ideas on how they should act; he asked for suggestions (for example, for the names of a character) but it was his task to decide whether they fitted or not with his plan. Rohmer chose his actors because of their optic and acoustic appearance, decided on their dresses, and—as Amanda Langlet says—often knew beforehand how they would interpret the screenplay (Cléder 2007: 59). All this is compatible with the integration of spontaneous gestures in his films, such as one of excuse by Arielle Dombasle after a fluff when she was asking to reshoot the scene (Cléder 2007: 63).

66 This does not imply that the actor should feel the same thing as the character he plays. An actor need not be angry in order to play anger well—herein Rohmer agrees with Diderot's *Paradoxe sur le comédien* (*The Paradox of Acting*) (2010: 164).

67 (2005), I 23–40; (1990), 63–80.

68 Similarly, Rohmer praises Rossellini's *Paisà (Paisan)* for having relied as little as possible on editing (1984: 34f.; 1989: 28) and criticizes those theorists who, like Eisenstein and André Malraux, put the essence of film in editing (2010: 167f.). He mentions also Balázs, to whom, however, he is closer than he thinks. See Balázs' criticism of Eisenstein's dualism of form and content, which sounds very Rohmerian (2001b: 164f.; 2010: 227). Also Arnheim is critical of the exaggerated importance of montage in Soviet film as well as of the inept categorization of montage by Vsevolod Pudovkin (1933: 94ff.; 2002: 95ff.). It is noteworthy that Arnheim's critique of overemphasizing montage is not based on a realist film theory—he argues that the single image has to be respected even before it enters montage, because it has already gone through a process of artistic transformation of nature.

69 Rohmer and Chabrol (1979), 96f. and (2011), 99.

70 See Leigh (2012), 219: "The shift to a close shot isolates her and suggests that her thoughts hold her apart from her husband and her family." I owe much to this excellent book, which, however, underrates the religious and philosophical dimensions of Rohmer's work.

71 This is a deliberate principle: Rohmer (2010), 121. Even the word "film," he claims, occurs only once, when the narrator wants to invite Jacqueline in the first of the sixteen films here discussed. Perhaps Rohmer was anxious about the potentially insidious nature of reflexivity.

72 Analogously, Hitchcock's criticism of the lecherous curiosity of people staring at the female corpse floating in the Thames in his penultimate feature film, *Frenzy*, is an indictment of his own public, and perhaps of himself.

73 (1984), 89.

74 (2010), 120f.

6: Content and Form in *Pauline à la plage*: Interweaving Words and Images

1 Almendros (1984), 267.

2 Rohmer himself for many years refused to own a phone.

3 On the incarnation of the contrast between the natural and the artificial in different characters of a film, see Bazin and Rohmer (1972), 121 and (1985), 87.

4 (2014), 265.

5 On the development of beach tourism, see Urbain (2002).

6 It is this scene that forms the center—the sixteenth of thirty-two according to one plausible counting (Leigh 2012: 115).

7 Henri is not seen in the same shot hovering above them, when Louisette and Sylvain are leaving—we only know from the earlier shot that Henri is standing in the upper floor. Uniting the three figures in a single shot would have been misleading, for Henri is not an equivalent of Michael but rather of a figure defeated by him according to Christian mythology.

8 Rohmer tells us that he likes to do things that nobody sees (2010: 122).

9 See Paul's *First Letter to the Corinthians* 15, 55f. It is tempting to relate Pauline's name to that of the first Christian theologian; and it is probably no accident either that the second best figure in the film, Pierre, too, has a name prominent in the New Testament.

10 See Rohmer and Chabrol (1979), 8 and (2011), 21f. Compare 148/149 on analogous scenes in *The Wrong Man*.

11 In the USA alone, it made more than $2.5 m (de Baecque and Herpe 2014: 316).

12 It might be that unconscious memories of Christian iconology contributed to the film's success, but I do not know how to test such a hypothesis.

13 In Plato's *Symposium* 221d, 7ff., Alcibiades speaks of the different levels in Socrates' speeches (and Plato through him on his own dialogues). It is not accidental that this important hermeneutical reflection is integrated into a discourse on love.

7: Rohmer the Non-Moralizing Moralist

1. (2010), 73. The early Schelling and Hegel would have loved this statement. See also p. 79 on the secret affinities of the flesh and the mind as manifested by the screen—one thinks of Schelling's definition of art as a synthesis of spirit and nature.

2. (2001a), 66f. and (2010), 52f.

3. Rohmer (2010), 56.

4. See Rohmer's important reflections on the difference between the metaphoric nature of individual elements that have been filmed, such as in Murnau, and the metaphor as a result of the montage, such as in Eisenstein (2010: 134f.). Needless to say, he prefers the former. But see Rohmer and Chabrol (1979), 132 and (2011), 134.

5. It would be a gratuitous objection to say that poetic justice occurs only in kitschy texts and films. For what marks such kitschy works is the complete arbitrariness of the stroke of luck that saves the good guys and punishes the bad ones. Rohmer, on the other hand, believes that there are psychological laws at work that explain why people sharing common values are more likely to bond or why lovers reserving the right to dump their beloveds may end up dumped themselves.

6. This distinguishes his films from the otherwise similarly realistic depiction of intimate life in Yasujirō Ozu. One may argue that death has become much rarer in the modern Western world among the age group Rohmer is interested in. The other great difference between Ozu and Rohmer—the impact of the parents on the marriage choices of their children—has to do with cultural differences between Japan and France in the twentieth century.

7. He and Chabrol discover in the idea of a community in sin one of the most important traits of Hitchcock's Christianity (1979: 114; 2011: 116).

8. (1988), 32: Rohmer speaks of "pure chance." See also Rohmer and Chabrol (1979), 113 and (2011), 115 on the divine signs appearing as workings of chance.

9. (1998a), 296ff.

10. (2010), 58. See also p. 74 on integrating evil into a system instead of condemning it.

8: Conclusion

1. The triple agent is Russian, his wife Greek. But here the internationalism is a result of the Russian aristocrat's exile. Furthermore, tsarist Russia and Greece were culturally relatively kindred. In the film, the Russian language is quite present, and subtitles are used (like at the end of *Conte d'automne*).

2. See (2010), 61. Compare p. 147. Balázs is no better (2001a: 22f.; 2010: 14f.).

3. This is rightly noted by Marocco (1996), 53 and 67. In their book on Hitchcock, Rohmer and Chabrol claim that homosexual love cannot be reciprocal (1979: 27f.; 2011: 41). But while this holds for the male character in *Murder!*, who is engaged to a woman only for convenience's sake, it does not necessarily apply to real homosexual love, whose difficulties have more often been a consequence of than a reason for social ostracism.

4. Alas, the child actress of Élise is not impressive. This is a pity, for Balázs is right that children have a peculiar affinity to film, since they see the world with fresh curiosity, as if in close-ups (2001a: 78f.; 2010: 62).

5. Mellen (1975), 149.

6. With reference to this film, Cardullo (2008: 136) speaks of Rohmer as a "women's director," for whom thought and speech are the true human action. And who would deny that women talk more than men?

7. One may compare her with Céladon, who stubbornly continues to love Astrée, who believes him dead. But the peak of his faithfulness is that he pretends to be a woman.

Bibliography

Almendros, Nestor (1980), *Un homme à la camera*, Paris: Hatier
Almendros, Nestor (1984), *A Man With a Camera*, New York: Farrar, Straus and Giroux
Anderst, Leah (2014), "Rohmer's Poetics of Placelessness," *The Films of Eric Rohmer. French New Wave to Old Master*, ed. Leah Anderst, Basingstoke and New York: Palgrave-Macmillan, 191–201
Arnheim, Rudolf (1933), *Film*, London: Faber & Faber
Arnheim, Rudolf (2002), *Film als Kunst*, Frankfurt: Suhrkamp
Baecque, Antoine de and Noël Herpe (2014), *Éric Rohmer*, Paris: Stock
Balázs, Béla (1952), *Theory of the Film (Character and Growth of a New Art)*, London: Dennis Dobson
Balázs, Béla (2001a), *Der sichtbare Mensch oder die Kultur des Films*, Frankfurt: Suhrkamp
Balázs, Béla (2001b), *Der Geist des Films*, Frankfurt: Suhrkamp
Balázs, Béla (2010), *Early Film Theory*, New York and Oxford: Berghahn
Bazin, André (1990), *Qu'est-ce que le cinéma?*, Paris: Les Éditions du Cerf
Bazin, André (2005), *What is Cinema?*, two vols, Berkeley: University of California Press
Bazin, André and Eric Rohmer (1972), *Charlie Chaplin*, Paris: Les Éditions du Cerf
Bazin, André, François Truffaut, Jean Renoir, and Eric Rohmer (1985), *Essays on Chaplin*, New Haven: University of New Haven Press
Biotti, Gabriele (2010), Luoghi del visibile moderno, Milano: Mimesis
Bonitzer, Pascal (1991), *Eric Rohmer*, Paris: Cahiers du Cinéma
Bozon, Michel, "Le hasard fait bien les choses. Sociologie de l'amour et du couple chez Éric Rohmer," *Informations Sociales* 144 (2007/08): 126–37
Cardullo, Bert (2008), *Five French Filmmakers: Renoir, Bresson, Tati, Truffaut, Rohmer; Essays and Interviews*, Newcastle-upon-Tyne: Cambridge Scholars Publishing

Carroll, Noël (1988), *Philosophical Problems of Classical Film Theory*, Princeton: Princeton University Press
Cavell, Stanley (1979), *The World Viewed. Reflections on the Ontology of Film*, Cambridge, MA, and London: Harvard University Press
Cavell, Stanley (2005), "On Eric Rohmer's *A Tale of Winter*," in *Cavell on Film*, ed. William Rothman, Albany: State University of New York Press, 287-93
Cervantes, Miguel de (1994), *El Ingenioso Hidalgo Don Quijote de la Mancha*, Madrid: Cátedra
Charney, Hanna, "Eric Rohmer's *Le genou de Claire*: Rousseau Revisited?," *Symposium* 27.2 (Summer 1973): 101-10
Cléder, Jean (2007), *Éric Rohmer. Évidence et ambiguïté du cinéma*, Lormont: Le Bord de l'Eau
Crisp, Colin G. (1988), *Eric Rohmer. Realist and Moralist*, Bloomington and Indianpolis: Indiana University Press
Flaubert, Gustave (1972), *Madame Bovary. Mœurs de province*, Paris: Gallimard
Fontane, Theodor (1969), *Frau Jenny Treibel*, München: Nymphenburger
Forster, Edward Morgan (1955), *Aspects of the Novel*, San Diego, New York and London: Harcourt Brace
Frampton, Daniel (2006), *Filmosophy*, London and New York: Wallflower
Goodman, Nelson (1976), *Languages of Art*, Indianapolis: Hackett
Guérin, Marie-Anne (2007), "Le miracle dans le champ: les rites et les exorcismes de l'amour mutuel chez Rohmer," *Rohmer et les Autres*, ed. Noël Herpe, Rennes: Presses Universitaires de Rennes, 85-94
Handyside, Fiona (2014), "Rohmer à la plage. The Role of the Beach in Three Films by Eric Rohmer," *French Cinema. Critical Concepts in Media and Cultural Studies*, ed. Phil Powrie, Vol. 2: *To the Nouvelle Vague*, London and New York: Routledge, 263-74
Hösle, Vittorio (2005), "Objective Idealism and Darwinism," *Darwinism & Philosophy*, ed. Vittorio Hösle and Christian Illies, Notre Dame: University of Notre Dame Press, 216-42
Hösle, Vittorio (2012), *The Philosophical Dialogue*, Notre Dame: University of Notre Dame Press
Hösle, Vittorio (2013), *The Many Faces of Beauty*, ed. Vittorio Hösle, Notre Dame: University of Notre Dame Press
Ingarden, Roman (1962), *Untersuchungen zur Ontologie der Kunst*, Tübingen: Niemeyer
Ingarden, Roman (1989), *Ontology of the Work of Art*, Athens, OH: Ohio University Press
Kierkegaard, Søren (1991), *Samlede Værker*, Copenhagen: Gyldendal
Laclos, Pierre Choderlos de (1964), *Les liaisons dangereuses*, Paris: Flammarion

Leigh, Jacob (2012), *The Cinema of Eric Rohmer*, London and New York: Continuum
Lewis, David, "Truth in Fiction," *American Philosophical Quarterly* 15 (1978): 37–46.
Lull, Ramon (1933), *Obres de Ramon Lull*, Vol. 17, Palma de Mallorca: Diputació Provincial de Balears
Marocco, Paolo (1996), *Eric Rohmer*, Recco-Genova: Le Mani
Mellen, Joan (1975), *Women and Their Sexuality in the New Film*, New York: Dell
Mullarkey, John (2009), *Refractions of Reality. Philosophy and the Moving Image*, Basingstoke and New York: Palgrave Macmillan
Panofsky, Erwin (1967), "Style and Medium in the Motion Pictures," *Film: An Anthology*, ed. Daniel Talbot, Berkeley: University of California Press, 15–32
Perkins, Victor F. (1972), *Film as Film: Understanding and Judging Movies*, Harmondsworth: Penguin
Robic, Sylvie (2013), "Le cinéma d'Éric Rohmer ou la transcendance comme un jeu," *Rohmer en perspectives*, ed. Sylvie Robic and Laurence Schifano, Paris: Presses Universitaires de Paris Ouest, 21–39
Roche, Mark (1997), *Tragedy and Comedy*, Albany: State University of New York
Rohmer, Éric (1974), *Six Contes Moraux*, Paris: L'Herne
Rohmer, Éric (1980), *Six Moral Tales*, London and New York: Lorrimer and Frederick Ungar
Rohmer, Éric (1984), *Le goût de la beauté*, Paris: Cahiers du Cinéma
Rohmer, Éric (1988), *Le Trio en mi bémol*, Paris: Actes Sud
Rohmer, Éric (1989), *The Taste for Beauty*, Cambridge: Cambridge University Press
Rohmer, Éric (1998a), *De Mozart en Beethoven, essai sur la notion de profondeur en musique*, Paris: Actes Sud
Rohmer, Éric (1998b), *Contes de quatre saisons*, Paris: Cahiers du Cinéma
Rohmer, Éric (1999), *Comédies et proverbes*, two vols, Paris: Cahiers du Cinéma
Rohmer, Éric (2000), *L'organisation de l'espace dans le Faust de Murnau*, Paris: Cahiers du Cinema
Rohmer, Éric (2007), *La maison d'Elisabeth*, Paris: Gallimard
Rohmer, Éric (2010), *Le celluloid et le marbre suivi d'un entretien inédit avec Noël Herpe et Philippe Fauvel*, Paris: Éditions Léo Scheer
Rohmer, Éric (2013), *Interviews*, ed. Fiona Handyside, Jackson: University Press of Mississippi
Rohmer, Éric and Claude Chabrol (1979), *The First Forty-Four Films*, New York: Frederick Ungar
Rohmer, Éric and Claude Chabrol (2011), *Hitchcock*, Paris: Éditions Ramsay

Rousseau, Jean-Jacques (1964), *Les Confessions*, Paris: Garnier
Sartre, Jean-Paul (1943), *L'Être et le néant*, Paris: Gallimard
Schilling, Derek (2007), *Eric Rohmer*, Manchester and New York: Manchester University Press
Serceau, Michel (2000), *Éric Rohmer. Les jeux de l'amour, du hasard et du discours*, Paris: Les Éditions du Cerf
Showalter, English (1993), *My Night at Maud's: Eric Rohmer, Director*, New Brunswick: Rutgers University Press
Sinnerbrink, Robert (2011), *New Philosophies of Film. Thinking Images*, London: Continuum
Sontag, Susan (1978), *Against Interpretation and Other Essays*, New York: Octagon
Sontag, Susan (1991), *Styles of Radical Will*, New York: Doubleday
Stendhal (1965), *De l'amour*, Paris: Flammarion
Tester, Keith (2008), *Eric Rohmer. Film as Theology*, Basingstoke and New York: Palgrave Macmillan
Tortajada, Maria (1999), *Le spectateur séduit*, Paris: Éditions Kimé
Urbain, Jean-Didier (2002), *Sur la plage. Mœurs et coutumes balnéaires (XIXe-XXe siècles)*, Paris: Payot

Index

12 Angry Men 117

À bout de souffle 123
abstract painting 153
acting 56, 104, 121, 122
Action Française 23
action, unity of 116–17
actionism 83
actors 112, 122
  amateur 66, 121
ad-libbing 122
adultery 38
Aeneid 36
aesthetic autonomy 121
aesthetic value 105, 106, 109
aestheticism 27, 112
aesthetics 153
  Hegelian 20
  music 151
afterimages 105
agnosticism 23
Alain 172
Allen, Woody xvii, xviii, 154
  Purple Rose of Cairo, The 107
  Zelig 168
Almendros, Néstor 25, 118, 131, 173, 174, 176
Ami de mon amie, L' 70–8, 92, 119, 134, 155

Amores 4, 163
amour fou 88
Amour l'après-midi, L' 38–43, 115, 107, 146
Amours d'Astrée et de Céladon, Les xv, 116
Anderst, Leah 173
Anglaise et le duc, L' xiv, xvi, 5–6, 155, 173
Anna Karenina 7
Annecy 31
Année dernière à Marienbad, L' 172
Apuleius
  Florida 174
Arbre, le maire et la médiathèque ou les sept hazards, L' xiv, 168
Arnheim, Rudolf 167, 171, 175
Arroseur Arrosé, L' 106
Ars Amatoria 4
asceticism 32
asymmetry 74, 100, 156, 157
atheism 23
Atkine, Féodor 128
Au hasard Balthazar 143
Auerbach, Erich
  Mimesis xv

Bach, Johann Sebastian 151
Bacon, Francis 118

Baecque, Antoine de 161, 163, 173, 174, 176
Balázs, Béla 145, 170, 172, 174, 175, 178
Balzac, Honoré de xi
Barrault, Marie-Christine 24, 163
Bauchau, Patrick 29
Bazin, André xi, 112, 113, 161, 167, 169, 171, 176
Beau mariage, Le 50–5, 78, 117, 156
Beaumarchais, Pierre 90
beauty 105, 117, 151
Beauvoir, Simone de 162
Beethoven, Ludwig van 151
Being and Time 51
Bennett, Éloise 84
Bergman, Ingmar
 Sommernattens leende 71
Berlin: Die Sinfonie der Großstadt 169
Berlin Film Festival 25, 128
Beuzen, Philippe 18
Bible 138
Biotti, Gabriele 172
Blackton, J. Stuart 169
Blouse Roumaine, La 141
body language 27, 110, 111, 122, 130, 135, 138
Bonitzer, Pascal 163, 165
Boudu sauvé des eaux 40
Bougainville, Louis Antoine de 39
 Le voyage autour du monde 165
Boulangère de Monceau, La 14–17
bourgeois drama 114
Bozon, Michel 171
Brave New World 142
Bresson, Robert xiv, 121, 171
 Au hasard Balthazar 143
 Pickpocket 154
Brialy, Jean-Claude 35, 121
Bronenosetz Potyomkin 110

budgets 121, 153
Bühler, Karl 170

Cahiers du Cinéma xi, xiii
Caillot, Haydée 50
camera 57, 68, 104, 109, 125, 130, 136–7
Camus, Albert 26
Capellanus, Andreas 4, 162
 De Amore 4, 162
capitalism 17
Caprices de Marianne, Les 6, 63, 64, 79–80
Caravaggio
 Musicians, The 125
Cardullo, Bert 178
Carrière, Mathieu 50
Carrière de Suzanne, La 14, 17–19
Carroll, Noël 167
Catholicism 7, 19–25, 100, 101, 143, 149, 152, 155
 sexual morality 148
Catullus 4
Cavell, Stanley 166, 173
Celluloid et le marbre, Le xiii
Chabrol, Claude xi, 162, 164, 171, 172, 174, 175, 176, 177, 178
Champaigne, Philippe de
 Christ mort couché sur son linceul 141
Chan, Neil 50
chance 93–4, 102
Chaplin, Charlie xi
 Countess from Hong Kong, A 161
Charney, Hanna 165
Chartier, Émile-Auguste 172
Chaulet, Emmanuelle 77
Chekhov, Anton 173
children 156
chivalry 4, 9
Chrétien de Troyes xv

Index

Christ mort couché sur son linceul 141
Christianity 4, 6, 20, 22, 100, 128, 137
   ethics 5
   iconography 137–8, 143
Christology 152
Ciarlet, Danièle 121
cinema 105, 113
   talking cinema 104
cinematography 25, 27, 68, 109, 123–4, 130, 136–7
class 16, 56
classicism 113
Cléder, Jean 175
Clermont-Ferrand 19
close-ups 110, 123, 124, 170, 178
clothes, *see also* costume 129, 135
co-expressibility 109
Cohl, Émile 169
Collectionneuse, La 25–30, 115, 118, 120, 146
color 79, 108, 118–19, 135
color film 118
Comédies et proverbes, see also individual films by name xv, 45–78
comedy 5, 55, 66, 71, 92, 98, 148
   classical 73
   New Comedy 156
   twin comedies 73
Commedia 67
commitment 34, 35, 37, 63, 80, 82
communication 111
   non-verbal 122
Communism 19
compassion 55
compliments 30
Comte, Auguste 23
condescendence 86, 130, 138, 139, 158

Confessions, Les 31
conscience 151
conscious 108, 125
Conte d'automne 39, 90–6, 124, 154–5, 178
Conte d'été xvii, 85–90, 117, 119, 131, 140, 165
Conte d'hiver 17, 96–102, 115, 116, 124, 163
Conte de printemps 8, 80–5, 117, 141
content 127–44
Contes de quatre saisons, see also individual films by name xv, xvii, 79–102
Contes moraux, see Six Contes moraux
contraceptives 9
conversation 122
Cornu, Aurora 32
Corot, Camille 173
costumes, *see also* clothes 125
   color 119
Countess from Hong Kong, A 161
coup de foudre 51, 57, 134
courtly love 87
courtship 122
creativity 153
Crisp, Colin 164, 165
culture 131
Cunningham, Frank R. 164
Cymbeline 96
Cynics 120

Dalí, Salvador 115
dance 110
Danish Dogme 95, 171
Dante
   Commedia 67
Daphnis and Chloe 38
Darel, Florence 84
Darwin, Charles 10, 106

De Amore 4, 162
De l'amour 6, 159, 165
De Mozart en Beethoven, essai sur la notion de profondeur en musique xiii
deconstruction 158
Dekalog 37
Deposition 143
dialogue 19, 45, 56, 83, 103, 104, 122, 132
　abstract 112
didacticism 55
Diderot, Denis
　Paradoxe sur le comédien 175
　Supplément au voyage de Bougainville 165
directors 123
Divine Institutes 174
divorce 23, 150
docu-fiction 168
documentary 112
Dombasle, Arielle 121, 128, 175
domination 157
Dostoyevsky, Fyodor
　Idiot, The 28, 69
drama, bourgeois 114
Dreyer, Carl Theodor 164
Driessche, Frédéric van den 98

ecologism 131
Eden 138
editing 104, 109, 123
Effi Briest 7
Eisenstein, Sergei 175, 177
　Bronenosetz Potyomkin 110
Élisabeth XII
elective affinities 70–8
Elliott, Grace xiv
Enten-Eller 7
Ermey, Ronald Lee 174
Erotes 3

erotic attraction 34, 93, 150
erotic behavior 47
erotic desire 30, 35
erotic exclusion 39
erotic loser 46–50
erotic love 38, 51, 154
erotic quadrilaterals 70–8, 79
erotic tension 92, 132
erotic triangles 72
eroticism 1–11, 154, 155, 159
Erotikos 3
eternal feminine 64
ethicotheology 100
ethics 8
　Christian 5
Être et le néant, L' 165
eurocentrism 155
Euthydemus 31
evolution, sexual 2
"Evolution of the Language of Cinema, The" 123
existentialism 26
expression, facial 110
expressionism 113
　German 112
extended shots 124

Fabian, Françoise 121, 163
facial expression 110
fairy tale 66
faith 101
Fall, the 131–44
family 3
family law 9
Faust 133
Fellini, Federico 164
female resistance 52
feminism 18, 156–7
Femme de l'aviateur, La 46–50, 117, 121, 125, 146
Fermat, Pierre 20

fictionality 106
film music 110
film theory
    feminist 156–7
filmmaking 113
Fitzcarraldo 114
flashbacks 116
Flaubert, Gustave
    Madame Bovary 6–7
Flight to Egypt 108
flirtation 14–19, 33, 39, 68, 75, 76, 92, 101, 111, 118, 123, 130, 135
Florida 174
Fonda, Henry 168
Fontane, Theodor 54–5, 165
    Effi Briest 7
    Frau Jenny Treibel 54–5
form 108, 127–44
formalism 27
Forms, theory of 151
Forster, E. M. 19
    Longest Journey, The 115
framing 124, 126
Frampton, Daniel 168
Frau Jenny Treibel 54–5
freeze-frame 124
Frenzy 176
Freud, Sigmund 9
friendship 34, 58, 62, 80, 95
Frygt og Bæven 102
Full Metal Jacket 174
full shots 123
Füssli, Johann Heinrich
    Nightmare, The 125

gallantry 30
Gauguin, Paul 125
gender 8–9, 28, 45, 64, 80, 156–8
    gender inversion 80
    relations 156
    roles 28
Gendron, François-Éric 77
Genesis 133
Geneva, Lake 32
Genou de Claire, Le 30–7, 56, 116, 118, 124, 125, 138, 149
genre 17
gestures 133
Gibbon, Edward 106
Gift of the Magi, The 166
gluttony 15, 16
Godard, Jean-Luc xii, 28, 123, 161
    À bout de souffle 123
    Mépris, Le 28
Goethe, Johann Wolfgang von 71, 101, 166, 170
    Wahlverwandtschaften, Die 71
    "Warum gabst du uns die tiefen Blicke" 101
    Wilhelm Meisters Wanderjahre 80
Goodman, Nelson 167
goodness 151, 152
grace 114
Grande Odalisque 126
Greggory, Pascal 128
Guérin, Marie-Anne 165
guilt 26

happy ending 55, 66
Hegel, Georg Wilhelm Friedrich xiii, 168, 177
    Aesthetics 20
Heidegger, Martin 51
    Being and Time 51
Henry, O.
    Gift of the Magi, The 166
hermeneutics 128
hermeticism 144
Heroides 4
Herpe, Noël 161, 163, 173, 174, 176
Herzog, Werner

Fitzcarraldo 114
Hiroshima mon amour 172
Hitchcock, Alfred xi, 115, 122, 154, 159, 162, 164, 172, 177, 178
   Frenzy 175
   Lodger, The 143
   Marnie 116
   Murder! 178
   Rope 174
   Spellbound 115
   Stage Fright 116
   Wrong Man, The 176
homoeroticism 155
homosexuality 3, 10, 155
human fragility 41
humanism 170
Hume, David 5
humiliation 76, 139, 157
humor 54, 86
Husserl, Edmund 8, 82
   Ideen zu einer reinen Phänomenologie und phänomenologischen Philosophie 169
Huxley, Aldous
   Brave New World 142

iconography, Christian 137–8, 143
iconology 141
Ideen zu einer reinen Phänomenologie und phänomenologischen Philosophie 169
Idiot, The 28, 69
Iliad 76, 173
imagery 131–44
improvisation 66, 122
incarnation 23
infatuation 88
Ingarden, Roman 108, 168, 169
Ingres, Dominique
   Grande Odalisque, La 126

intellectualism 27
intermediality 166
internationalism 155
intertextuality 66
intimacy 26
intuition 75

Jansenism 20, 141, 143
Japan 155
jealousy 18, 47, 48, 59, 87
Jesus Christ 134, 141, 142, 143, 152
   Deposition 143
Journey to Italy 146
Julie, ou la nouvelle Héloïse 5, 32
Juno 38–43
justice 9

Kant, Immanuel xiii, 82, 100, 120, 164
   aesthetics of music 151
Käthchen von Heilbronn, Das 162
Keaton, Buster
   Seven Chances 168
Kierkegaard, Søren 7, 20, 57
   Enten-Eller 7
   Frygt og Bæven 102
   Stadier på Livets Vej 7, 165
Kieślowski, Krzysztof 114
   Dekalog 37
kitschy works 177
Kleist, Heinrich von xv
   Käthchen von Heilbronn, Das 162
Kogan, Leonid 120
Körkarlen 154
Kracauer, Siegfried 167
Kritik der Urteilskraft 174
Kubrick, Stanley
   Full Metal Jacket 174
Kuleshov effect 169
Kurosawa, Akira
   Rashomon 172

Index

La Brosse, Simon de 129
La Rochefoucauld, François de la 159
Laclos, Pierre Choderlos de 163
   Liaisons dangereuses, Les 5–6
Lactantius
   Divine Institutes 174
Langlet, Amanda xvii, 61, 89, 128, 175
language 110, 111
   spoken 111
law of impermeability 170
Le Mans
   cathedral 53
Lecas, Gérard 139
Leda 33
Leibniz, Gottfried Wilhelm 152
Leigh, Jacob 175, 176
Leone, Sergio
   Once Upon a Time in the West 168
Lewis, David 169
Liaisons dangereuses, Les 5–6
liberalism, secular 19
Libolt, Alain 94
light 119
lighting 125
literature 108
Llull, Ramon
   Art amativa 166
location 80, 92
Lodger, The 143
loneliness 67
long shots 123
long takes 123
Longest Journey, The 115
Longus
   Daphnis and Chloe 38
Louvre 126
love triangles 72
Luchini, Fabrice 64, 65, 121
Lumet, Sidney

12 Angry Men 117
Lumière, Louis 168
Lumière brothers 106
   Arroseur Arrosé, L' 106
lust 15
Lycée Henri-IV 172
Lysis 3

Ma nuit chez Maud 19–25, 37, 116, 118, 120, 124, 143–4, 156, 163
Madame Bovary 6–7
Maison d'Elisabeth, La 161
Malraux, André 175
Mann, Thomas
   Zauberberg, Der 146
Marie of France, Countess of Champagne 162
Marocco, Paolo 178
Marivaux, Pierre de 5
Marnie 116
Marquise von O…, Die xv, 107, 125
marriage 2–3, 4–5, 14, 18, 32, 46, 50–5, 63, 70, 71, 150
Marx, Groucho 36
Marxism 45
masculinity 100
matchmaking 79, 92, 93, 96
Matisse, Henri
   Blouse Roumaine, La 141
Maurras, Charles
   Action Française 23
medicine 9
medium shots 123
Mellen, Joan 156, 178
Mépris, Le 28
metaphor 145, 146
metaphysics 8
metatheater 96
metempsychosis 100
Meury, Anne-Laure 50
Midsummer Night's Dream, A 71

Mimesis xv
miracles 102
mirrors 115, 118, 126
mise-en-scène 132
mockumentary 168
Monaghan, Laurence de 35, 122
Mont Saint-Michel 136
montage 137
Montaigne, Michel de 4, 38
    Sur des vers de Virgile 4
Monzat, Denis xv
moral instinct 159
moralism 151, 152
morality 60
Mosjoukine, Ivan 169
Mozart, Wolfgang Amadeus 151
Mullarkey, John 168
Murder! 178
Murnau, F. W. xi, 113, 164, 172, 174, 177
    Faust 133
    Tabu 119
music 109, 110, 120, 121
    aesthetics of 151
Musicians, The 125
Musil, Robert 39
Musset, Alfred de 6, 66
    Caprices de Marianne, Les 6, 63, 64

Nanterre 162
narcissism 25–30, 34, 36, 115, 146
narrations 116
narrator 158
    gender 158
natural light 118
natural selection 2
naturalism 143, 151
nature 120, 130, 131
Neorealism 112
Neorealists 121, 148

New Comedy 156
New Hollywood xi
Nietzsche, Friedrich 32, 36
Nietzscheanism 164
Nightmare, The 125
noise pollution 120
Nouvelle Vague xi, xv, 123, 153
novellas 103
nudity 119, 126, 134
Nuits de la pleine lune, Les 61–6, 72, 80, 86, 117

Ogier, Pascale 65
Old Testament 134
Once Upon a Time in the West 168
ontology 106
"Ontology of the Photographic Image, The" 167
opportunism 159
Out 1: Noli me tangere xi
Ovid 4, 5, 10
    Amores 4, 163
    Ars Amatoria 4
    Heroides 4
    Remedia Amoris 4
ovulation 2
ownership 63
Ozu, Yasujirō 177

painting 108, 124, 125
    abstract 153
"Painting and Cinema" 169
Paisà 175
panning shots 123, 137
Panofsky, Erwin 110, 168
pantomime 110
Paris 15, 47, 64
"Paris m'a séduit" 121
partialism 30, 154
Pascal, Blaise 20, 159, 164
passion-love 47

Paul 176
Pauline à la plage xvii, 17, 23, 33, 48, 55–61, 117, 127–44, 146, 154
   biblical allusions 127
   iconology 141
   plot 128
Perceval le Gallois xv, 171
Pericles 96
Perkins, Victor 167
perspectivity 108
petite bourgeoisie 98
petite maison 62
Petites filles modèles, Les 166
petitionary prayer 53
Petrarch 33
Phaedrus 3
phantasies 10, 38, 40, 115
   revenge 140
   sexual 132
phenomenology 8
phi phenomena 105
philosophy, transcendental 82–3
photography 105, 107, 113
Physiognomics 170
Picasso, Pablo 124
Pickpocket 154
Plato 31, 82, 101
   dialogues 3, 112
   Euthydemus 31
   Lysis 3
   Phaedrus 3
   Symposium 3, 176
   theory of Forms 151
   Timaeus 113
Plautus
plot 103
Plutarch
   Erotikos 3
poetic justice 147, 148
poetry, erotic 3
point of view 106

politeness 41
Politoff, Haydée 29
portraiture 118
possessiveness 59
Poupaud, Melvil 89
"Pour un cinéma parlant" 104
prayer, petitionary 53
Prix Méliès 128
probability theory 20
production companies 121
prohibition, sexual 9
projection 75
promiscuity 25–30, 140
Propertius 4
Provence 27
Pseudo-Aristotle 170
Pseudo-Lucian, *Erotes* 3
Pudovkin, Vsevolod 175
Purple Rose of Cairo, The 107

Quatre Aventures de Reinette et Mirabelle 120, 165
Quatre cents coups, Les 131
Quéré, Françoise 129
Quester, Hugues 84

Rashomon 115, 172
Rayon vert, Le 66–70, 118, 119, 122, 131, 154
realism 103–26, 145, 151, 153
redemption 131–44
reflection 45
Règle du jeu, La 6, 63, 64
reincarnation 101
religion 22, 23, 45, 100, 101–2, 127, 133
religiosity 53, 152, 160
Remedia Amoris 4
Renan, Ernest 151
Rendez-vous de Paris, Les 74, 117
Renoir, Jean 66, 162

Boudu sauvé des eaux 40
Règle du jeu, La 6, 63, 64
Renoir, Sophie 77
representation 120
reproduction 3
resentment 36
Resnais, Alain
   Année dernière à Marienbad, L' 172
   Hiroshima mon amour 172
   Smoking/No Smoking 172
revenge 50, 59
   phantasies 140
Richardson, Tony
   Tom Jones 15
rights 62
Rimbaud, Arthur 69
Rivette, Jacques
   Out 1: Noli me tangere xi
Rivière, Marie 67, 70, 94, 98, 121
Robic, Sylvie 163
Roche, Mark 166
romance 98
Romand, Béatrice 54
Romanticism 6
Rope 174
Rossellini, Roberto 112
   Journey to Italy 146
   Paisà 192
Rousseau, Jean-Jacques 5, 31, 45, 165, 173
   Confessions, Les 31
   Julie, ou la nouvelle Héloïse 5, 32, 165
Rousseausism 30–7
Ruttmann, Walter
   Berlin: Die Sinfonie der Großstadt 169

Sade, Marquis de 6
Sartre, Jean-Paul 26, 31, 162, 164

Être et le néant, L' 165
satire 27
Scheler, Max 8, 20, 36
   Zur Phänomenolige und Theorie der Sympathiegefühle 8
Schelling, Friedrich Wilhelm Joseph xiii, 177
Schérer, Denis xv
Schérer, Mathilde 161
Scherer, Max 164
Schiller, Friedrich 164
Schillig, Derek 174
Schleger, Friedrich 32
Schopenhauer, Arthur xiii, 9, 120
Schroeder, Barbet 16
screenplay 66
secular liberalism 19
seduction 10–11, 18, 29, 38, 52, 55–61, 64, 81, 83–4
Sée, Catherine 18
self-awareness 53
self-criticism 53
self-deception 55, 146
self-delusion 157
self-respect 52
self-sacrifice 102
semantics 107
sensual love 47
sensuality 26
Serceau, Michel 165, 166
sex scenes 119
sexual behavior 2
sexual desire 146, 147
sexual drive 8, 123
sexual evolution 2
sexual needs 58
sexual prohibition 9
sexual revolution 10
sexual selection 2
sexual tension 87
sexuality 29, 143

Index

Shakespeare, William 66, 73, 96–8, 100, 154, 166, 170
   Cymbeline 96
   Midsummer Night's Dream, A 71
   Pericles 96
   Tempest, The 96
   Winter's Tale, The 96
Showalter, English 164
Signe du lion, Le 89
silent film 104, 107, 108, 109, 110, 111, 124
sin 25, 142, 150
Sinnerbrink, Robert 161
Six Contes Moraux see also individual films by name xv, 13–43, 81, 114, 115, 157, 164
Sjöströms, Victor
   Körkarlen 154
Smoking/No Smoking 172
sociality 68
Sommernattens leende 71
Sontag, Susan 167, 171
sound 110, 111, 120
space, unity of 117
speech 104
speech acts 111
Spellbound 115
Spinoza, Baruch 82
spoken language 111
Stadier på Livets Vej 7, 165
Stage Fright 116
star system 112, 121
Steiner, George 149
Stendhal 47
   De l'amour 6, 159, 165
strategy 90
stream of consciousness 27, 76, 108
structure 72, 103, 117, 158
subtitles 110
Supplément au voyage de Bougainville 165

supranatural 100
Sur des vers de Virgile 4
symmetry 74
Symposium 3, 176

tableau vivant 126
Tabu 119
talking 112
talking cinema 104, 111
technology 10, 145
telling on others 30–7
Tempest, The 96
temporality 57
Temps Modernes, Les 161
Terra trema, La 168
Tester, Keith 162
Teyssèdre, Anne 84
theater 104, 108
thing-in-itself 120, 151
Tibullus 4
Timaeus 113
time, unity of 116
Tolstoy, Leo
   Anna Karenina 7
Tom Jones 15
Tortajada, Maria 172
Tous les garçons s'appellent Patrick 20
transcendentalism 83
translation 171
Trier, Lars von 171
Trintignant, Jean-Louis 24, 121, 163, 164
Trio en mi bémol, Le 163, 166
Triple Agent xvi, 124, 147
Tristan und Isolde 143
Truffaut, François xi, 131
   Quatre cents coups, Les 131
twins 73–4

unconscious 125

unfaithfulness 62–3
unity of action 116–17
unity of space 117
unity of time 116
unreliability of narrator 163
Urbain, Jean-Didier 176
Urfé, Honoré d' xv–xvi, 173

vacation sex 69
vanity-love 47
Venus 38–43
Verley, Bernard 42
Verne, Jules 66, 69
Véry, Charlotte 98
victimhood 17
Viellard, Éric 77
Vinterberg, Thomas 171
Virgil
    Aeneid 36
virility 90
Visconti, Luchino
    Terra trema, La 168

Vitez, Antoine 163
Voyage autour du monde, Le 165
voice-over 13, 19, 45, 111
voyeurism 37, 47, 125

Wagner, Richard
    Tristan und Isolde 143
    Wahlverwandtschaften, Die 71
Walker, Beverly 164
Warens, Françoise-Louise 31–2
Wilhelm Meisters Wanderjahre 80
Will 120
Winter's Tale, The 96
women 123, 156–7, 159
    emancipation 8
    idealization 4
Wrong Man, The 176

Zauberberg, Der 146
Zelig 168
Zur Phänomenolige und Theorie der
    Sympathiegefühle 8

Made in the USA
Las Vegas, NV
02 February 2021